IS MILITAF
ACTION JL
AGAINST NATIONS
THAT SUPPORT
TERRORISM?

IS MILITARY ACTION JUSTIFIED AGAINST NATIONS THAT SUPPORT TERRORISM?

Other books in the At Issue series:

IS MILITARY ACTION JUSTIFIED AGAINST NATIONS THAT SUPPORT TERRORISM?

James D. Torr, *Book Editor*

Daniel Leone, *President*
Bonnie Szumski, *Publisher*
Scott Barbour, *Managing Editor*
Helen Cothran, *Senior Editor*

GREENHAVEN
PRESS ®

San Diego • Detroit • New York • San Francisco • Cleveland
New Haven, Conn. • Waterville, Maine • London • Munich

LIBRARY OF CONGRESS CATALOGING-IN-PUBLICATION DATA

Is military action justified against nations thought to support terrorism? / James D. Torr, book editor.
    p. cm. — (At issue)
Includes bibliographical references and index.
ISBN 0-7377-1833-1 (pbk. : alk. paper) — ISBN 0-7377-1832-3 (lib. : alk. paper)
    1. Terrorism—Government policy—United States—Public opinion. 2. War on Terrorism, 2001—Public opinion. 3. National security—United States—Public opinion. 4. Public opinion—United States. I. Torr, James D., 1974– . II. At issue (San Diego, Calif.)
HV6432.I672 2003
363.3'2—dc21

2002041628

Contents

Introduction

Perhaps the most controversial issue surrounding terrorism is how governments should respond to it. This controversy stems from the dual nature of terrorism—it has both criminal and military aspects. In countering terrorism, governments must deal with criminals—often murderers—who may have the organization, sophistication, and capacity for violence of a military force. Effective counterterrorism, therefore, often consists of both traditional law enforcement techniques and military operations.

A good example of the law enforcement approach was the U.S. government's response to the bombing of the World Trade Center in New York City on February 26, 1993, an attack that killed 6 people and injured more than 1,000 others. FBI agents handled the investigation of the bombing, and four assistant U.S. attorneys were put in charge of the prosecution. The FBI quickly apprehended 4 suspects with ties to Islamic fundamentalist groups, who were then tried and sentenced to 240 years in prison on May 25, 1994. In 1995, the alleged mastermind behind the bombing, Ramzi Yousef, was arrested in Pakistan, and a sixth conspirator was arrested in Jordan. In 1998, both men were also given 240-year sentences.

The United States has used a much different approach in responding to the terrorist attacks of September 11, 2001, that destroyed the same World Trade Center complex that had been targeted in 1993 and killed more than 3,000 people. In an address to the nation just hours after the attacks, President George W. Bush warned that "our military is powerful, and it's prepared." He also promised that the United States would "make no distinction between the terrorists who committed these acts and those who harbor them." Moreover, in pledging the United States to an ongoing "war on terrorism," President Bush made it clear that U.S. counterterrorism efforts will be broader in scope than ever before and may rely much more on the use of military force than they have in the past.

State-sponsored terrorism

In contrast to the 1993 bombers, the terrorists who hijacked four airplanes on the morning of September 11 made no attempt to escape; instead, they perished along with their victims. When it was learned that the 19 hijackers had belonged to the al Qaeda terrorist network—a group led by Osama bin Laden and based largely in Afghanistan—President Bush re-emphasized that America's response to September 11 would include targeting states that condone terrorism. On September 20, 2001, he warned that "every nation, in every region, now has a decision to make. Either you are with us, or you are with the terrorists." A month later, he declared, "Every nation has a choice to make. In this conflict, there is no neutral ground. If any government sponsors the outlaws and killers of innocents, they have become outlaws and murderers, themselves. And they will take that lonely path at their own peril."

Bush's statements were directed in part at the Taliban, the fundamentalist Muslim regime in Afghanistan that had harbored al Qaeda. But Bush also framed his statements as part of a larger campaign against terrorism, a campaign he vowed would go beyond capturing bin Laden or destroying the al Qaeda network. Deputy Secretary of Defense Paul Wolfowitz tried to clarify Bush's position: "It's not just simply a matter of capturing people and holding them accountable, but removing the sanctuaries, removing the support systems, ending states who sponsor terrorism." He added, "And that's why it has to be a broad and sustained campaign. It's not going to stop if a few criminals are taken care of."

A new kind of war?

Even in the emotional aftermath of September 11 there were some dissenters who did not share in the widespread support for the war on terrorism. Quentin Peel, the editor of London's *Financial Times*, questioned the very concept of state-sponsored terrorism in a September 28 editorial:

> Terrorism . . . does not need the resources of an identifiable government. It does not even need much of a base. In the modern age, it is highly mobile . . . Its agents live in London, Hamburg, Florida, you name it. The search for state sponsors may therefore prove to be dangerously irrelevant. . . . The only way to fight terrorism in the long term is to fight the causes of terrorism. That means tackling the misery and despair in countries such as Afghanistan. It means striving with every means available to bring peace to the Middle East.

Peel continued, "The danger of declaring war on terrorism is that it implies using the overwhelming power of the US . . . to crush the organisations espousing terrorism. But that will not remove the tactic of terrorism from the armoury of the desperate. If anything, it will reinforce its use as the only possible weapon."

Critics of the war on terrorism have not only questioned the effectiveness of using military force against states thought to support terrorism, but also the morality of this approach. As Peel puts it, "How does one define the US practice of aerial bombardment from 30,000ft? Absolute accuracy cannot be guaranteed and civilian casualties are inevitable. . . . Does it not amount to terror tactics, even if some might say they were justified?" In their October 29, 2001, issue, the editors of the *Nation* emphasized that "Military actions inside Afghanistan must be circumscribed by limited political objectives and carried out with a minimum of civilian casualties."

In preparing for and while conducting the Operation Enduring Freedom—as the invasion of Afghanistan was called—U.S. officials, well aware of dissenters' concerns, emphasized how new, sophisticated targeting mechanisms and other weapons technologies would help minimize civilian casualties in Afghanistan. In addition, Secretary of Defense Donald Rumsfeld claimed that the United States intends to target governments that sponsor terrorism and not the people living under those regimes. In a September 27 *New York Times* article titled "A New Kind of War," Rumsfeld wrote, "Our opponent is a global network of terrorist organizations and their state sponsors, committed to denying free people the opportunity to live as they choose. While we may engage militarily against foreign governments that sponsor terrorism, we may also seek to make allies of the people these governments oppress."

Throughout Operation Enduring Freedom, which resulted in the removal of the Taliban from power (but not the capture of Osama bin Laden), critics and supporters of the war on terrorism debated whether the war in Afghanistan was being waged in a just manner. Meanwhile, U.S. leaders prepared Americans and the international community for future engagements.

The Bush doctrine

In its May 2001 report, *Patterns of Global Terrorism*, the U.S. Department of State listed seven countries that the United States suspects of harboring or sponsoring terrorists before September 11: Cuba, Iran, Iraq, Libya, North Korea, Sudan, and Syria. In his January 29, 2002, State of the Union address, President Bush made it clear that the war on terrorism would not end in Afghanistan:

> What we have found in Afghanistan confirms that, far from ending there, our war against terror is only beginning. Most of the 19 men who hijacked planes on September 11th were trained in Afghanistan's camps, and so were tens of thousands of others. Thousands of dangerous killers, schooled in the methods of murder, often supported by outlaw regimes, are now spread throughout the world. . . . So long as training camps operate, so long as nations harbor terrorists, freedom is at risk.

Bush went on to discuss the threat that weapons of mass destruction—chemical, nuclear, or biological—could pose in the hands of terrorists, and to single out three nations in particular as targets in the war on terrorism:

> [We must] prevent regimes that sponsor terror from threatening America or our friends and allies with weapons of mass destruction. . . . North Korea is a regime arming with missiles and weapons of mass destruction, while starving its citizens. Iran aggressively pursues these weapons and exports terror, while an unelected few repress the Iranian people's hope for freedom. Iraq continues to flaunt its hostility toward America and to support terror. . . . States like these, and their terrorist allies, constitute an axis of evil, arming to threaten the peace of the world. By seeking weapons of mass destruction, these regimes pose a grave and growing danger. They could provide these arms to terrorists, giving them the means to match their hatred . . . The United States will not permit the world's most dangerous regimes to threaten us with the world's most destructive weapons.

While much of the public continued to support the war on terrorism, the prospect of a perpetual military campaign drew criticism from pacifists and human rights activists, as well as from those who thought President Bush was exceeding the limits of presidential authority. As the editors of the *Progressive* railed:

> Bush views himself as unfettered by Congress or the Constitution to wage his worldwide campaign against terrorists and regimes that sponsor terrorism. In the first sentence of his State of the Union address, he declared "Our nation is at war," but he never asked or received a formal declaration of war from Congress. And when Congress gave him authorization to use force in September [2001], it said that such use of force had to be limited to individuals, groups, or nations connected to the attacks of September 11. Congress did not give him carte blanche to wage war against any and all terrorists everywhere, or against regimes that seek chemical, biological, or nuclear weapons.

Moreover, political analysts were divided over whether Bush's labeling of North Korea, Iran, and Iraq as an "axis of evil" was justified or overly aggressive.

The debate over whether the United States should use military force against these nations became particularly intense when, at a speech at West Point on June 1, 2002, President Bush spoke of the need to strike pre-emptively at terrorist threats. "If we wait for threats to materialize, we will have waited too long. . . . We must take the battle to the enemy, disrupt his plans, and confront the worst threats before they emerge," he warned. On the one hand, Bush's remarks echoed the consensus in the counterterrorism community that because it is impossible to defend against every possible terrorist attack, a more effective policy is to identify and neutralize terrorists threats before they are carried out. On the other hand, critics worried how the "Bush doctrine" of pre-emption—as it was soon dubbed—would be applied to states thought to support terrorism. As a *Time* editorial put it:

> It . . . seems as if the U.S. has arrogated to itself the right to go to war whenever it sniffs danger from a regime it doesn't like. . . . What happens if other nations follow the lead of the U.S. and incorporate pre-emption into their strategic thinking? (Imagine nuclear-armed India deciding to attack terrorist camps in nuclear-armed Pakistan.) That way lies international anarchy.

Controversy over the Bush doctrine also revived long-standing foreign policy debates over whether the United States should act unilaterally to protect U.S. interests or multilaterally in accordance with the United Nations.

Military action against Iraq

The controversy resulting from President Bush's remarks at West Point was due in part to rumors that had been circulating in the media for months—rumors that the Bush administration intended to invade Iraq and remove dictator Saddam Hussein from power. Some foreign policy "hawks" cheered the idea, arguing that Iraq harbored an arsenal of biological and chemical weapons and was a chief sponsor of global terrorism. So-called "doves" countered that there was not enough evidence to support these charges, and contended that for the United States to invade Iraq without UN approval would be a violation of international law.

On September 12, 2002, President Bush made his case against Iraq before the UN General Assembly, summarizing the Iraqi government's human rights violations against its own people as well as its history of non-compliance with UN weapons inspections that were imposed on Iraq after the 1991 Persian Gulf War. Throughout the following winter, the Bush administration argued that Iraq was harboring weapons of mass destruction in violation of UN resolutions and that "regime change" was needed. However, U.S. proposals to forcibly depose Saddam Hussein met with sharp resistance from key UN members, including France, Russia, and Germany. On March 17, 2003, in a televised address, President Bush announced that the United States would invade Iraq despite opposition within the UN:

> No nation can possibly claim that Iraq has disarmed. And it will not disarm so long as Saddam Hussein holds power. . . . Yet, some permanent members of the Security Council have publicly announced they will veto any resolution that compels the disarmament of Iraq. These governments share our assessment of the danger, but not our resolve to meet it. . . . We are now acting because the risks of inaction would be far greater. In one year, or five years, the power of Iraq to inflict harm on all free nations would be multiplied many times over.

America's conflict with Iraq is one aspect of the broader issue of what role military force should play in countering state-sponsored terrorism. Military action against Iraq will be the next phase of the war on terrorism, but it is not likely to be the last. As President Bush noted on the first anniversary of the September 11 attacks, "America has entered a great struggle that tests our strength, and even more our resolve." The viewpoints in *At Issue: Is Military Action Justified Against Nations Thought to Support Terrorism?* discuss America's case against Iraq as well as the broader ethical issues involved in using military force to deter terrorism.

1

The Terrorist Attacks on America Justify the Use of Military Force Against States That Support Terrorism

George W. Bush

George W. Bush is the forty-third president of the United States.

The events of September 11, 2001, demonstrated to the world the evil of terrorism; but September 11 will also be remembered as the day that the nations of the world resolved to fight this evil. In the six months since September 11, Operation Enduring Freedom—the U.S.-led military occupation of Afghanistan—has been largely successful in its efforts to destroy the al Qaeda terrorist network. However, terrorism is a global problem and will require a global response. The nations of the world must work to expose and apprehend terrorists and confront governments that harbor terrorists with diplomatic ultimatums, and if necessary, military force.

Editor's note: President Bush issued the following remarks on the White House lawn in commemoration of the six-month anniversary of the September 11, 2001, terrorist attacks on America.

Diplomatic representatives of the coalition of nations; members of the Congress, the Cabinet, the Supreme Court; members of the American Armed Forces; military coalition members from around the world; distinguished guests; and ladies and gentlemen. Welcome to the White House.

We have come together to mark a terrible day, to reaffirm a just and vital cause, and to thank the many nations that share our resolve and will share our common victory.

George W. Bush, "Six-Month Anniversary of the September 11th Attacks," *Vital Speeches of the Day*, vol. 68, April 1, 2002.

Six months separate us from the September 11th [terrorist attacks on America]. Yet, for the families of the lost, each day brings new pain; each day requires new courage. Your grace and strength have been an example to our nation. America will not forget the lives that were taken, and the justice their death requires.

We face an enemy of ruthless ambition, unconstrained by law or morality. The terrorists despise other religions and have defiled their own. And they are determined to expand the scale and scope of their murder. The terror that targeted New York and Washington could next strike any center of civilization. Against such an enemy, there is no immunity, and there can be no neutrality.

Time for reckoning

Many nations and many families have lived in the shadows of terrorism for decades—enduring years of mindless and merciless killing. September the 11th was not the beginning of global terror, but it was the beginning of the world's concerted response. History will know that day not only as a day of tragedy, but as a day of decision—when the civilized world was stirred to anger and to action. And the terrorists will remember September 11th as the day their reckoning began.

A mighty coalition of civilized nations is now defending our common security. Terrorist assets have been frozen. Terrorist front groups have been exposed. A terrorist regime has been toppled from power. Terrorist plots have been unraveled, from Spain to Singapore. And thousands of terrorists have been brought to justice, are in prison, or are running in fear of their lives. With us today are representatives from many of our partners in this great work, and we're proud to display their flags at the White House this morning. From the contributions these nations have made—some well known, others not—I am honored to extend the deepest gratitude of the people of the United States.

September 11th was not the beginning of global terror, but it was the beginning of the world's concerted response.

The power and vitality of our coalition have been proven in Afghanistan [during the war to topple the reigning Taliban regime]. More than half of the forces now assisting the heroic Afghan fighters, or providing security in Kabul, are from countries other than the United States. There are many examples of commitment: our good ally, France, has deployed nearly one-fourth of its navy to support Operation Enduring Freedom, and Great Britain has sent its largest naval task force in 20 years. British and American special operations forces have fought beside teams from Australia, Canada, Norway, Denmark and Germany. In total, 17 nations have forces deployed in the region. And we could not have done our work without critical support from countries, particularly like Pakistan and Uzbekistan.

Japanese destroyers are refueling coalition ships in the Indian Ocean.

The Turkish air force has refueled American planes. Afghans are receiving treatment in hospitals built by Russians, Jordanians, Spanish, and have received supplies and help from South Korea. Nations in our coalition have shared in the responsibilities and sacrifices of our cause. On the day before September the 11th, I met with Prime Minister John Howard of Australia, who spoke of the common beliefs and shared affection of our two countries. We could not have known that bond was about to be proven again in war, and we could not have known its human cost. Last month, Sergeant Andrew Russell of the Australian Special Air Service died in Afghanistan. He left behind his wife, Kylie, and their daughter, Leisa, just 11 days old. Friends said of Sergeant Russell, "You could rely on him never to let you down."

This young man, and many like him, have not let us down. Each life taken from us is a terrible loss. We have lost young people from Germany and Denmark and Afghanistan and America. We mourn each one. And for their bravery in a noble cause, we honor them. Part of that cause was to liberate the Afghan people from terrorist occupation, and we did so. Next week, the schools reopen in Afghanistan. They will be open to all— and many young girls will go to school for the first time in their young lives. Afghanistan has many difficult challenges ahead—and, yet, we've averted mass starvation, begun clearing mine fields, rebuilding roads and improving health care. In Kabul, a friendly government is now an essential member of the coalition against terror.

Now that the Taliban are gone and [the terrorist organization] al Qaeda has lost its home base for terrorism, we have entered the second stage of the war on terror—a sustained campaign to deny sanctuary to terrorists who would threaten our citizens from anywhere in the world.

In Afghanistan, hundreds of trained killers are now dead. Many have been captured. Others are still on the run, hoping to strike again.

These terrorist fighters are the most committed, the most dangerous, and the least likely to surrender. They are trying to regroup, and we'll stop them. For five months in Afghanistan, our coalition has been patient and relentless. And more patience and more courage will be required. We're fighting a fierce battle in the Shahi-kot Mountains, and we're winning. Yet, it will not be the last battle in Afghanistan. And there will be other battles beyond that nation.

For terrorists fleeing Afghanistan—for any terrorist looking for a base of operations, there must be no refuge, no safe haven. By driving terrorists from place to place, we disrupt the planning and training for further attacks on America and the civilized world. Every terrorist must be made to live as an international fugitive, with no place to settle or organize, no place to hide, no governments to hide behind, and not even a safe place to sleep.

A global coalition

I have set a clear policy in the second stage of the war on terror: America encourages and expects governments everywhere to help remove the terrorist parasites that threaten their own countries and peace of the world. If governments need training, or resources to meet this commitment, America will help.

We are helping right now in the Philippines, where terrorists with links to al Qaeda are trying to seize the southern part of the country to establish a militant regime. They are oppressing local peoples, and have kidnapped both American and Filipino citizens. America has sent more than 500 troops to train Philippine forces. We stand with President Gloria Arroyo, who is courageously opposing the threat of terror.

For America, the war on terror is not just a policy, it's a pledge.

In the Republic of Georgia, terrorists working closely with al Qaeda operate in the Pankisi Gorge near the Russian border. At President Edvard Shevardnadze's request, the United States is planning to send up to 150 military trainers to prepare Georgian soldiers to reestablish control in this lawless region. This temporary assistance serves the interests of both our countries.

In Yemen, we are working to avert the possibility of another Afghanistan. Many al Qaeda recruits come from near the Yemen–Saudi Arabian border, and al Qaeda may try to reconstitute itself in remote corners of that region. President Ali Abdullah Saleh has assured me that he is committed to confronting this danger. We will help Yemeni forces with both training and equipment to prevent that land from becoming a haven for terrorists.

In the current stage of the war our coalition is opposing not a nation, but a network. Victory will come over time, as that network is patiently and steadily dismantled. This will require international cooperation on a number of fronts: diplomatic, financial and military. We will not send American troops to every battle, but America will actively prepare other nations for the battles ahead. This mission will end when the work is finished—when terror networks of global reach have been defeated. The havens and training camps of terror are a threat to our lives and to our way of life, and they will be destroyed.

The threat of state-sponsored terrorism

At the same time, every nation in our coalition must take seriously the growing threat of terror on a catastrophic scale—terror armed with biological, chemical, or nuclear weapons. America is now consulting with friends and allies about this greatest of dangers, and we're determined to confront it.

Here is what we already know: some states that sponsor terror are seeking or already possess weapons of mass destruction; terrorist groups are hungry for these weapons, and would use them without a hint of conscience. And we know that these weapons, in the hands of terrorists, would unleash blackmail and genocide and chaos. These facts cannot be denied, and must be confronted. In preventing the spread of weapons of mass destruction, there is no margin for error, and no chance to learn from mistakes. Our coalition must act deliberately, but inaction is not an option. Men with no respect for life must never be allowed to control the ultimate instruments of death.

Gathered here today, we are six months along—a short time in a long struggle. And our war on terror will be judged by its finish, not by its start. More dangers and sacrifices lie ahead. Yet, America is prepared. Our resolve has only grown, because we remember. We remember the horror and heroism of that morning—the death of children on a field trip, the resistance of passengers on a doomed airplane, the courage of rescuers who died with strangers they were trying to save. And we remember the video images of terrorists who laughed at our loss.

Every civilized nation has a part in this struggle, because every civilized nation has a stake in its outcome. There can be no peace in a world where differences and grievances become an excuse to target the innocent for murder. In fighting terror, we fight for the conditions that will make lasting peace possible. We fight for lawful change against chaotic violence, for human choice against coercion and cruelty, and for the dignity and goodness of every life.

America's pledge

Every nation should know that, for America, the war on terror is not just a policy, it's a pledge. I will not relent in this struggle for the freedom and security of my country and the civilized world.

And we'll succeed. There will be a day when the organized threat against America, our friends and allies is broken. And when the terrorists are disrupted and scattered and discredited, many old conflicts will appear in a new light—without the constant fear and cycle of bitterness that terrorists spread with their violence. We will see then that the old and serious disputes can be settled within the bounds of reason and goodwill and mutual security. I see a peaceful world beyond the war on terror, and with courage and unity, we are building that world together.

Any nation that makes an unequivocal commitment against terror can join this cause. Every nation of goodwill is welcome. And, together, we will face the peril of our moment, and seize the promise of our times.

May God bless our coalition.

2

The Terrorist Attacks on America Do Not Justify the Use of Military Force Against States That Support Terrorism

Larry Mosqueda

Larry Mosqueda is a professor of society, politics, behavior, and change at Evergreen State College in Washington State.

The September 11, 2001, terrorist attacks on America were horrific, but the U.S. government has committed many acts of violence around the globe that could also be labeled as "terrorism." U.S. policies and military actions have killed millions of civilians since World War II. In the wake of September 11, the U.S. government has announced its intent to wage war on governments that may be complicit in terrorism. This policy will result in yet more slaughter of civilians who have little or no influence over their undemocratic governments' actions. A better policy would be to deal with terrorists as individual criminals and to work to reduce the economic and social conditions that give rise to terrorism.

L ike all Americans, I was shocked and horrified to watch the World Trade Center (WTC) Twin Towers attacked by hijacked planes and collapse, resulting in the deaths of thousands of innocent people [on September 11, 2001].

I had not been that shocked and horrified since January 16, 1991, when then President George H. Bush attacked Baghdad, and the rest of Iraq and began killing 200,000 people during that "war" (slaughter). This includes the infamous "highway of death" in the last days of the slaughter when US pilots literally shot in the back retreating Iraqi civilians and soldiers. I continue to be horrified by the sanctions on Iraq, which have

Larry Mosqueda, "Shocked and Horrified," *Synthesis/Regeneration*, Winter 2002. Copyright © 2002 by *Synthesis/Regeneration*. Reproduced by permission.

resulted in the death of over 1,000,000 Iraqis, including over 500,000 children, about whom former Secretary of State Madeleine Albright has stated, their deaths "are worth the cost."

America's atrocities

Over the course of my life I have been shocked and horrified by a variety of US governmental actions, such as the US sponsored coup against democracy in Guatemala in 1954 which resulted in the deaths of over 120,000 Guatemalan peasants by US installed dictatorships over the course of four decades.

Events of September 11 reminded me of the horror I felt when the US overthrew the government of the Dominican Republic in 1965 and helped to murder 3,000 people. And it reminded me of the shock I felt in 1973, when the US sponsored a coup in Chile against the democratic government of Salvador Allende and helped to murder another 30,000 people, including US citizens.

Events of September 11 reminded me of the shock and horror I felt in 1965 when the US sponsored a coup in Indonesia that resulted in the murder of over 800,000 people, and the subsequent slaughter in 1975 of over 250,000 innocent people in East Timor by the Indonesian regime, with the direct complicity of President Gerald Ford and Secretary of State Henry Kissinger.

I was reminded of the shock and horror I felt during the US sponsored terrorist contra war (the World Court declared the US government a war criminal in 1984 for the mining of the harbors) against Nicaragua in the 1980s which resulted in the deaths of over 30,000 innocent people (or as the US government used to call them before the term "collateral damage" was invented—"soft targets").

I was reminded of being horrified by the US war against the people of El Salvador in the 1980s, which resulted in the brutal deaths of over 80,000 "soft targets."

I was reminded of the shock and horror I felt during the US sponsored terror war against the peoples of southern Africa (especially Angola) that began in the 1970s and continues to this day, and has resulted in the deaths and mutilations of over 1,000,000. I was reminded of the shock and horror I felt as the US invaded Panama over the Christmas season of 1989 and killed over 8,000 in an attempt to capture George H. Bush's CIA partner, now turned enemy, Manuel Noriega.

A conservative number for those who have been killed by US terror and military action since World War II is 8,000,000 people.

I was reminded of the horror I felt when I learned about how the Shah of Iran was installed in a US sponsored brutal coup that resulted in the deaths of over 70,000 Iranians from 1952–1979. And the continuing shock as I learned that the Ayatollah Khomeini, who overthrew the Shah in 1979 and who was the US public enemy for the decade of the 1980s was also on the CIA payroll while he was in exile in Paris in the 1970s.

I was reminded of the shock and horror that I felt as I learned how the US has "manufactured consent" since 1948 for its support of Israel, to the exclusion of virtually any rights for the Palestinians in their native lands. I was shocked as I learned about the hundreds of towns and villages that were literally wiped off the face of the earth in the early days of Israeli colonization. I was horrified in 1982 as the villagers of Sabra and Shatila were massacred by Israeli allies with direct Israeli complicity and direction. The untold thousands who died on that day match the scene of horror that we saw on September 11. But those scenes were not repeated over and over again on the national media to inflame the American public.

Of course, the largest and most shocking war crime of the second half of the 20th century was the US assault on Indochina from 1954–1975, especially Vietnam, where over 4,000,000 people were bombed, napalmed, crushed, shot and individually "hands on" murdered in the "Phoenix Program" (this is where Oliver North got his start). Many US Vietnam veterans were also victimized by this war and had the best of intentions, but the policy makers themselves knew the criminality of their actions and policies as revealed in their own words in "The Pentagon Papers."

I was continually shocked and horrified as the US attacked and bombed with impunity the nation of Libya in the 1980s, including killing the infant daughter of Khadafi. I was shocked as the US bombed and invaded Grenada in 1983. I was horrified by US military and CIA actions in Somalia, Haiti, Afghanistan, Sudan, Brazil, Argentina, and Yugoslavia. The deaths in these actions ran into the hundreds of thousands.

Putting September 11 in context

The above list is by no means complete or comprehensive. It has just been conveniently eliminated from the public discourse and public consciousness. And for the most part, the analysis that the US actions have resulted in the deaths of primarily civilians (over 90%) is not unknown to the elites and policy makers. A conservative number for those who have been killed by US terror and military action since World War II is 8,000,000 people. This does not include the wounded, the imprisoned, the displaced, the refugees, etc.

Nothing that I have written is meant to disparage or disrespect those who were victims and those who suffered death or the loss of a loved one during [the September 11 attacks]. It is not meant to "justify" any action by those who bombed the Twin Towers or the Pentagon. It is meant to put it in a context.

Ed Herman in his book *The Real Terror Network: Terrorism in Fact and Propaganda* does not justify any terrorism but points out that states often engage in "wholesale" terror, while those whom governments define as "terrorist" engage in "retail" terrorism. And the seeds of much of the "retail" terror are in fact found in the "wholesale" terror of states. Again this is not to justify, in any way, the actions of September 11, but to put them in a context and suggest an explanation.

Perhaps most shocking and horrific, if indeed [terrorist Osama] bin Laden is the mastermind of the actions of September 11, he has clearly had significant training by competent and expert military personnel. During the 1980s, he was recruited, trained and funded by the CIA in Afghanistan to fight against the Russians. As long as he visited his terror on Russians and his enemies in Afghanistan, he was "our man" in that country.

The same is true of Saddam Hussein of Iraq, who was a CIA asset in Iraq during the 1980s. Hussein could gas his own people, repress the population, and invade his neighbor Iran as long as he did it with US approval.

We should not allow ourselves to [turn] real grief and anger into a national policy of wholesale terror and genocide against civilians in Asia and Africa.

The same was true of Manuel Noriega of Panama, who was a contemporary and CIA partner of George H. Bush in the 1980s. Noriega's main crime for Bush, the father, was not that he dealt drugs (he did, but the US and Bush knew this before 1989), but that Noriega was no longer going to cooperate in the ongoing US terrorist contra war against Nicaragua. This information is not unknown or really controversial among elite policy makers. To repeat, this is not to justify any of the actions of September 11, but to put it in its horrifying context.

Isolated acts of terror do not justify wholesale war

As shocking as the events of September 11 were, they are likely to generate even more horrific actions by the US government that will add significantly to the 8,000,000 figure stated above. This response may well be qualitatively and quantitatively worse than the events of Tuesday, September 11. The *New York Times* headline of 9/14/01 states that, "Bush And Top Aides Proclaim Policy of Ending States That Back Terror" as if that was a rational, measured, or even sane option. States that have been identified for possible elimination are "a number of Asian and African countries, like Afghanistan, Iraq, Sudan, even Pakistan." This is beyond shocking and horrific—it is just as potentially suicidal, homicidal, and more insane than the hijackers themselves.

The retail terror is that of desperate and sometimes fanatical small groups and individuals who often have legitimate grievances, but engage in individual criminal and illegitimate activities; the wholesale terror is that of "rational" educated men where the pain, suffering, and deaths of millions of people are contemplated, planned, and too often executed, for the purpose of furthering a nebulous concept called the "national interest." Space does not allow a full explanation of the elites' Orwellian concept of the "national interest," but it can be summarized as the protection and expansion of hegemony and an empire.

The American public is being prepared for war while being fed a continuous stream of shocking and horrific repeated images of the events of September 11, and heartfelt stories from the survivors and the loved ones of those who lost family members. These stories are real and should not be diminished. In fact, those who lost family members can be considered a representative sample of the 8,000,000 who have been lost previously. If we multiply by 800–1000 times the amount of pain, angst, and anger being currently felt by the American public, we might begin to understand how much of the rest of the world feels as they are continually victimized.

Some particularly poignant images are the heart-wrenching public stories that we are seeing and hearing of family members with pictures and flyers searching for their loved ones. These images are virtually the same as those of the "Mothers of the Disappeared" who searched for their (primarily) adult children in places such as Argentina, where over 11,000 were "disappeared" in 1976–1982, again with US approval. Just as the mothers of Argentina deserved our respect and compassion, so do those who are searching for their relatives now. However we should not allow ourselves to be manipulated by the media and US government into turning real grief and anger into a national policy of wholesale terror and genocide against innocent civilians in Asia and Africa. What we are seeing, in military terms is called "softening the target." The target here is the American public and we are being ideologically and emotionally prepared for the slaughter.

None of the previously identified Asian and African countries are democracies, which means that the people of these countries have virtually no impact on developing the policies of their governments, even if we assume that these governments are complicit in the actions of September 11. When one examines the recent history of these countries, one will find that the American government had direct and indirect influences on creating the conditions for the existence of some of these governments. This is especially true of the Taliban government of Afghanistan itself.

End the horror

If there is a great war, the crimes of that war will be revisited upon the US over the next generation. That is not some kind of religious prophecy or threat, it is merely a straightforward political analysis. If indeed it is bin Laden, the world must not deal only with him as an individual criminal, but eliminate the conditions that create the injustices and war crimes that will inevitably lead to more of these types of attacks in the future. The phrase "No Justice, No Peace" is more than a slogan used in a march, it is an observable historical fact. It is time to end the horror.

3

The United States Should Go to War Against Nations That Support Terrorism

Angelo M. Codevilla

Angelo M. Codevilla is a professor of politics and international relations at Boston University and a senior fellow at the Claremont Institute, a conservative think tank.

In the wake of the September 11, 2001, terrorist attacks on America, the United States has touted increased homeland security measures and better intelligence operations as the preferred means of winning the war on terror. However, common sense dictates that victory in war means destroying the enemy. In the war on terror, the enemy is not Islam or even terrorist networks like al Qaeda. Rather, the enemy is the regimes in Iraq and Syria, as well as the Palestinian Liberation Authority, that train, finance, and harbor terrorists and promote anti-Western sentiments. These regimes, and not the people they rule over, are America's enemies, much as the Nazi government, and not the German people, was America's enemy in World War II. Destroying pro-terror regimes is the best and most just means of winning the war on terror.

As Americans mourned on the night of September 11 [2001, after the terrorist attacks], many in the Middle East celebrated. Their enemies, 280 million people disposing of one third the wealth of the earth, had been bloodied. Better yet, Americans were sadly telling each other that life would never be the same as before—and certainly not better.

The revelers' joy was troubled only by the fear that an angry America might crush them. For a few hours, Palestinian warlords referred to the events as Al Nachba—"the disaster"—and from Gaza to Baghdad the order spread that victory parties must be out of sight of cameras and that any inflammatory footage must be seized. But soon, to their relief, the revelers heard the American government announce that it would not hold them responsible. President George W. Bush gratuitously held out

Angelo M. Codevilla, "Victory," *Human Events*, vol. 57, December 3, 2001. Copyright © 2001 by *Human Events*. Reproduced by permission.

the cachet of "allies" in the war on terrorism to nations that the U.S. government had officially designated as the world's chief sponsors of terrorism. Thus [Palestinian leader] Yasser Arafat's, [Iraqi leader] Saddam Hussein's, and [Syrian president] Bashar al Assad's regimes could enjoy, undisturbed, the success of the anti-Western cause that alone legitimizes their rule. That peace is their victory, and our lack of peace is our defeat.

What victory means

Common sense does not mistake the difference between victory and defeat: the losers weep and cower, while the winners strut and rejoice. The losers have to change their ways, the winners feel more secure than ever in theirs. On September 12, retiring Texas Senator Phil Graham encapsulated this common sense: "I don't want to change the way I live. I want to change the way they live." Common sense says that victory means living without worry that some foreigners might kill us on behalf of their causes, but also without having to bow to domestic bureaucrats and cops, especially useless ones. It means not changing the tradition by which the government of the United States treats citizens as its masters rather than as potential enemies. Victory requires killing our enemies, or making them live in debilitating fear. . . .

Our peace, our victory, requires bloody vengeance for the murder of some 5,000 innocent family members and friends—we seek at least as many deaths, at least as gory, not to appease our Furies, nor even because justice requires it. Vengeance is necessary to eliminate actual enemies, and to leave no hope for any person or cause inimical to America. Killing those people, those hopes, and those causes is the sine qua non of our peace—and very much within our power.

Fortunately, our peace, our victory, does not require that the peoples of Afghanistan, the Arabian Peninsula, Palestine, or indeed any other part of the world become democratic, free, or decent. They do not require any change in anybody's religion. We have neither the power nor the right to make such changes. Nor, fortunately, does our peace depend on making sure that others will like us. We have no power to make that happen. Neither our nor anyone else's peace has ever depended on creating "New World Orders," "collective security," or "communities of power." International relations are not magic. Our own peace does not depend on any two foreign governments being at peace with each other. It is not in our power or in the power of any third party to force such a peace except by making war on both governments. Much less does our peace depend on a "comprehensive peace" in the Middle East or anywhere else. It is not in our power to make such a peace except by conquering whole regions of the world. Our peace and prosperity do not depend on the existence of friendly regimes in any country whatever, including Saudi Arabia. That is fortunate, because we have no power to determine "who rules" in any other country.

Virtually all America's statesmen until Woodrow Wilson warned that the rest of mankind would not develop ideas and habits like ours or live by our standards. Hence we should not expect any relief from the permanent burdens of international affairs, and of war. Indeed, statesmen from George Washington to Abraham Lincoln made clear that any attempt to dictate another people's regime or religion would likelier result in resentment abroad and faction at home than in any relief from foreign troubles. We can and must live permanently in a world of alien regimes and religions. The mere difference in religion or mode of government does not mean that others will trouble our peace, whether or not any foreign rulers make or allow war on America is a matter of their choice alone. We can talk, negotiate, and exercise economic pressure on rulers who trouble our peace. But if they make war on us we have no choice but to make war on them and kill them. Though we cannot determine who will rule, we surely can determine who will neither rule nor live.

Victory requires killing our enemies, or making them live in debilitating fear.

What do we want from the Middle East to secure our peace? Neither democracy nor a moderate form of Islam—only that the region's leaders neither make nor allow war on us, lest they die. We have both the right and the capacity to make sure of that. But is it not necessary for our peace that the countries of the region be ruled by regimes friendly to us? No. By all accounts, the Saudi royal family's personal friendship with Americans has not affected their aiding and abetting terror against us. It is necessary only that any rulers, whatever their inclinations might be, know that they and their entourages will be killed, surely and brutally, if any harm to Americans originates from within their borders. Respect beats friendship. Do we not have to make sure that the oil of the Middle East continues to fuel the world economy? Is this not necessary to our peace? Indeed. But this does not burden us with the impossible task of ensuring that Saudi Arabia and the Oil States are ruled by friendly regimes. We need only ensure that whoever rules those hot sands does not interfere with the production of the oil that lies beneath them. That we can do, if we will.

In sum, ending the war that broke out on September 11 with our peace will require a lot of killing—to eliminate those in any way responsible for attacking us, and those who might cause further violence to us or choke the world's economy by troubling the supply of oil. It turns out that these mostly are the same persons. Who then are the enemies whose deaths will bring us peace?

It's the regime, stupid

When the suicide pilots of September 11 died, they made nonsense of the notion that terrorism was perpetrated by and on behalf of "senseless" individuals, and that the solution to terrorism lay in "bringing to justice" the bombers and trigger pullers. If this notion were adhered to, the fact that the terrorists had already gone to justice should have ended the matter, except for some ritual exhortation to states to be a bit more careful about madmen in their populations.

But these terrorists were neither madmen nor on the edges of society. They came from well-established families. They had more than casual contacts with the political movements and intelligence services of their own regime and of neighboring countries. They acted on behalf of international causes that are the main sources of legitimacy for some regimes of the Middle East, and are tolerated by all. These causes include a version of Islam; a version of Arab nationalism; driving Westerners and Western influence from Islamic lands; and ridding the Arab world of more or less pro-Western regimes like that of Egypt, Saudi Arabia, and the [United Arab] Emirates. Moreover, peoples and regimes alike cheered their acts. In short, these acts were not private. Rather, they were much like the old Western practice of "privateering" (enshrined in Article I of our own Constitution, vide "letters of Marque and Reprisal"), in which individuals not under formal discipline of governments nevertheless were chartered by governments to make war on their behalf.

Since the terrorists of September 11 are dead and we sense that their deeds were not merely on their own behalf but rather that they acted as soldiers, the question imposes itself: Whose soldiers? Who is responsible? Whose death will bring us peace?

Islam is not responsible. It has been around longer than the United States, and coexisted with it peacefully for two hundred years. No doubt a version of Islam—Islamism—a cross between the Wahabi sect and secular anti-Westernism, is central to those who want to kill Americans. But it is neither necessary nor sufficient nor possible for Americans to enter into intra-Muslim theological debates. Besides, these debates are not terribly relevant. The relevant fact is that the re-definition of Islam into something harmful to us is the work of certain regimes and could not survive without them.

Rulers [should] know that they and their entourages will be killed, surely and brutally, if any harm to Americans originates from within their borders.

Regimes are forms of government, systems of incentives and disincentives, of honors and taboos and habits. Each kind of regime gives prominence to some kinds of people and practices, while pushing others to the margins of society. Different regimes bring out different possibilities inherent in the same people. Thus the Japanese regime prior to World War II changed the meaning of the national religion of Shinto from quaint rituals to militant emperor-worship. Germany meant vastly different things to the German people and to the world when it was under the regime established by Konrad Adenauer, rather than the one established by Adolf Hitler. In short, regimes get to define themselves and the people who live under them.

Note that Palestine's Yasser Arafat, Iraq's Saddam Hussein, and Syria's Assad family have made themselves the icons of Islamism despite the fact that they are well known atheists who live un-Muslim lives and have persecuted unto death the Muslim movements in their countries. Nevertheless, they represent the hopes of millions for standing up to Westerners, driving Israel (hated more for its Westernness than its Jewishness) out of the Holy Land, and undoing the regimes that stand with the West. These tyrants represent those hopes because they in fact have managed to do impressive anti-Western deeds and have gotten away with it. The Middle East's memory of the Gulf War is that Saddam tried to drive a Western lackey out of Kuwait and then withstood the full might of America, later to spit in its face. The Middle East's view of Palestine is that Arafat and the Assads champion the rights of Islam against the Infidels.

Iraq, Syria, and the [Palestinian Liberation Organization] are the effective cause of global terrorism.

Nor are the Arab peoples or Arab nationalism necessarily our enemies. America coexisted peacefully with Arabs for two centuries. Indeed, the United States is largely responsible for pushing Britain and France to abandon colonial and neo-colonial rule over Arab peoples in the 1950s. U.S. policy has been unfailingly—perhaps blindly—in favor of Arab nationalism. It is true that Egypt's Gamal Abdul Nasser founded Arab nationalism on an anti-American basis in the 1950s. It is true that in 1958 the Arab Socialist Party's (Ba'ath) coup in Iraq and Syria gave Arab nationalism a mighty push in the anti-American direction. It is true that the Soviet Union and radical Arabs created the Palestine Liberation Organization [PLO] as an anti-Western movement. But it is also true that Jordan, Saudi Arabia, the Emirates, and, since 1973, Egypt have been just as Arab and just as nationalistic, though generally more pro-Western.

How did the PLO and the Ba'ath regimes of Syria and Iraq gather to themselves the mantle of Arab nationalism? First, the Saudis and the Emirates gave them money, while Americans and Europeans gave them respect and money. Saudis, Americans and Europeans gave these things in no small part because the radical Arabs employed terrorism from the very first, and Saudi, American, and European politicians, and Israelis as well, hoped to domesticate the radicals, buy them off, or divert them to other targets—including each other. Second and above all, we have given them victories, which they have used as warrants for strengthening their hold on their peoples and for recruiting more terrorists against us.

Today, Iraq, Syria, and the PLO are the effective cause of global terrorism. More than half of the world's terrorism since 1969, and nearly all of it since the fall of the Soviet Union, has been conducted on behalf of the policies and against the enemies of those three regimes. By comparison, Libya, Iran, and Sudan have been minor players. Afghanistan is just a place on the map. Factor these three malefactors out of the world's political equation, and what reason would any Arab inclined to Islamism or radical nationalism have to believe that such causes would stand a chance of success? Which intelligence service would provide would-be terrorists with the contacts, the money, the training to enter and fight the West or Israel? For whom, in short, would they soldier?

The Iraqi, Syrian, and the PLO regimes are no more true nationalists than they are true Muslims. They are regimes of a party, in the mold of the old Soviet Union. Each is based on a narrow segment of society and rules by physically eliminating its enemies. Iraq is actually not a nation-state but an empire. The ruling Ba'ath party comes from the Mesopotamian

Sunni Arabs, the smallest of the empire's three ethnic groups. The ruling faction of the party, Saddam's Tikriti, are a tiny fraction of the ruling party. The Assad family that rules Syria is even more isolated. The faction of the local Ba'ath party that is their instrument of power is made up almost exclusively of Alewites, a neo-Islamic sect widely despised in the region. It must rely exclusively on corrupt, hated security forces. Yasser Arafat rules the PLO through the Fatah faction, which lives by a combination of buying off competitors with money acquired from the West and Israel, and killing them. Each of the regimes consists of some 2,000 people. These include officials of the ruling party, officers in the security forces down to the level of colonel, plus all the general officers of the armed forces. These also include top government officials, officials of the major economic units, the media, and of course the leaders of the party's "social organizations" (labor, youth, women's professional, etc.).

All these regimes are weak. They have radically impoverished and brutalized their peoples. A few members of the ruling party may be prepared to give their lives for the anti-Western causes they represent, but many serve out of fear or greed. The Gulf War and the Arab-Israeli wars proved that their armies and security forces are brittle: tough so long as the inner apparatus of coercion is unchallenged, likely to disintegrate once it is challenged.

Killing these regimes would be relatively easy, would be a favor to the peoples living under them, and is the only way to stop terrorism among us.

On killing regimes

It follows that killing regimes means killing their members in ways that discredit the kinds of persons they were, the ways they lived, the things and ideas to which they gave prominence, the causes they espoused, and the results of their rule. Thus the Western Allies de-Nazified Germany not by carpet-bombing German cities, which in fact was the only thing that persuaded ordinary Germans that they and the Nazis were in the same boat. The Allies killed the Nazi regime by killing countless Nazis in battle, hanging dozens of survivors, imprisoning hundreds, and disqualifying thousands from social and economic prominence. The Allies promised to do worse to anyone who tried Nazism again, left no doubt in the minds of Germans that their many sorrows had been visited on them by the Nazis, and made Nazism into a dirty word.

Clearly, it is impossible to kill any regime by killing its people indiscriminately. In the Gulf War, U.S. forces killed uncounted tens of thousands of Iraqis whose deaths made no difference to the outcome of the war and the future of the region, while consciously sparing the much smaller number who made up the regime. Hence those who want to "bomb the hell out of the Arabs" or "nuke Baghdad" in response to September 11 are making the same mistake. Killing must be tailored to political effect. This certainly means invading Iraq, and perhaps Syria, with ground troops. It means openly sponsoring Israel's invasion of the PLO territories. But it does not mean close supervision or the kind of political reconstruction we performed in Germany and Japan after World War II.

It is important that U.S. forces invade Iraq with the stated objective of hanging Saddam and whoever we judge to have been too close to him.

Once those close to him realize that this is going to happen and cannot be stopped, they will kill one another, each trying to demonstrate that he was farther from the tyrant than anyone else. But America's reputation for bluff and for half measures is so entrenched that the invasion will have to make progress greater than in the Gulf War in order for this to happen. At this point, whether or not Saddam himself falls into U.S. hands alive along with his subordinates, it is essential that all be denounced, tried, and hanged on one charge only: having made war on America, on their own people, and on their neighbors. The list of people executed should follow the party-government's organization chart as clearly as possible. It is equally essential that everyone who hears of the event be certain that something even more drastic would follow the recrudescence of such a regime. All this should happen as quickly as possible.

Killing [the regimes that support terrorism] would be relatively easy, would be a favor to the peoples living under them, and is the only way to stop terrorism among us.

After settling America's quarrel, America should leave Iraq to the peoples who live there. These would certainly break the empire into its three ethnic constituents: Kurds in the North, Mesopotamian Sunnis in the center, and Marsh Shiites in the South. How they may govern themselves, deal with one another and with their neighbors, is no business of ours. What happens in Iraq is simply not as important to us as the internal developments of Germany and Japan were. It is enough that the Iraqis know that we would be ready to defend whatever interest of ours they might threaten. Prestige is a reputation for effective action in one's own interest. We would have re-earned our prestige, and hence our right to our peace.

In the meantime, we should apologize to Israel for having pressured her to continue absorbing terrorist attacks. We should urge Israel to act decisively to earn her own peace, which would involve destroying the regime of the PLO in the West Bank and Gaza. Israel could do this more easily than we could destroy Saddam's regime in Iraq. The reason is that the regime of the PLO, the so-called Palestine Liberation Authority (PLA), is wholly dependent on Israel itself for most basic services, from money and electricity to telecommunications, water, food, and fuel. Moreover, the PLA's key people are a few minutes' driving distance from Israeli forces. A cutoff of essentials, followed by a military cordon and an invasion, would net all but a few of these terrorists. The U.S. could not dictate how they should be disposed of. But it would make sense for Israel to follow the formula that they deserve death for the harm these criminal gangs have done to everyone with whom they have come in contact, even one another. With the death of the PLO's gangsters, Palestinian politics would be liberated from the culture of assassination that has stunted its healthy growth since the days of Mufti Hussein in the 1920s.

After Iraq and Palestine, it would be Syria's turn. By this time, the seriousness of America and its allies would speak for itself. A declaration of war against the Assad regime by the U.S., Israel, and Turkey would most likely produce a palace coup in Damascus—by one part of the regime eager to save itself by selling out the others—followed by a revolution in the country. At that point, the Allies might produce a list of persons who would have to be handed over to avert an invasion. And of course Syrian troops would have to leave Lebanon. Americans have no interest in Syria strong enough to require close supervision of successors to Assad. But Turkey's interest might require such supervision. The U.S. should make no objection to Turkey's reestablishment of a sphere of influence over parts of its former empire.

Destroying the major anti-Western regimes in the Middle East might come too late to save the moribund government of Saudi Arabia from the anti-Western sentiments that it has shortsightedly fostered within itself. Or the regime might succumb anyway to long-festering quarrels within the royal family. In any case, it is possible that as a consequence of the Saudi regime's natural death, the foreigners who actually extract and ship the oil might be endangered. In that case, we would have to choose among three options: 1) letting the oil become the tool of whoever might win the struggle (and taking the chance that the fields might be sabotaged in the war); 2) trying to build a new Saudi regime to our liking; or 3) taking over protection of the fields. The first amounts to entrusting the world's economy to the vagaries of irresponsible persons. The second option should be rejected because Americans cannot govern Arabs, or indeed any foreigners. Taking over the oil fields alone would amount to colonial conquest alien to the American tradition. It would not be alien, however, to place them under joint international supervision—something that Russia might well be eager to join.

Our own worst enemies?

What stands in the way of our achieving the peace we so desire? Primarily, the ideas of Western elites. Here are a few.

Violence and killing do not settle anything. In fact they are the ultima ratio, the decisive argument, on earth. Mankind's great questions are decided by war. The battle of Salamis decided whether or not there would be Greek civilization. Whether Western Europe would be Christian or Muslim was decided by the battle of Tours. Even as the U.S. Civil War decided the future of slavery and World War II ended Nazism, so this war will decide not just who rules in the Middle East, but the character of life in America as well.

Our primary objective in war as in peace must be to act in accordance with the wishes and standards of the broadest slice of mankind. In fact, the standards of most of mankind are far less worthy than those prevalent in America. America's Founders taught this, and forgetting it has caused harm. Alliances must always be means, never ends in themselves, and as such must be made or unmade according to whether or not they help secure our interest. Our interest in war is our kind of peace. That is why it is mistaken to consider as an ally anyone who impedes the killing of those who stand in the way of our peace. With allies like Saudi Arabia, America does not need enemies.

When involved in any conflict, we should moderate the pursuit of our objectives so as to propitiate those moderates who stand on the sidelines. Individuals and governments stand on the sidelines of conflict, or lend support to one side, according to their judgment of who will win and with whom they will have to deal. "Extremist" is one of many pejorative synonyms for "loser." The surest way to lose the support of "moderates" is to be ineffective. Might is mistaken for right everywhere, but especially in the Middle East. Hence the easiest way to encourage terrorism is to attempt to deal with "the root causes of resentment against us" by granting some of the demands of our enemies.

Learning to put up with security measures will make us safer, and is a contribution we can all make to victory. On the contrary, security measures will not make us safe, and accustoming ourselves to them is our contribution to defeat. The sign of victory over terrorism will be the removal of security measures.

The Arab regimes that are the matrices of terrorism have nothing going for them except such Western shibboleths. Their peoples hate them. Their armies would melt before ours as they have melted before Western armies since the days of Xenophon's Upcountry March. They produce nothing. Terror is their domestic policy and their foreign policy.

The regimes that are killing us and defeating us are the product of Western judgments in the mid-20th century that colonialism is wrong and that these peoples could govern themselves as good stewards of the world's oil markets. They continue to exist only because Western elites have judged that war is passe.

It is these ideas and judgments, above all, that stand in the way of our peace, our victory.

4

The United States Should Not Go to War Against Nations That Support Terrorism

Howard Zinn

Howard Zinn is a professor of history at Boston University and a colum-nist for the Progressive.

Terrorist acts such as those that occurred on September 11, 2001, are crimes against humanity, but so is America's "war on terror-ism." America's invasion of Afghanistan will kill far more civil-ians—largely because of intense bombing of Afghanistan's most populous areas—than did the September 11 attacks. Such killing of innocents, whether through terrorism or war, can never be jus-tified. Rather than expanding its military presence throughout the world, the United States should withdraw troops from the Middle East and increase humanitarian aid to the region.

Editor's note: The following selection was written in November 2001, when the U.S.-led military occupation of Afghanistan was getting underway.

I believe two moral judgments can be made about the present "war": The September 11, 2001, terrorist attack constitutes a crime against hu-manity and cannot be justified, and the bombing of Afghanistan [in or-der to rout the terrorist-harboring Taliban regime] is also a crime, which cannot be justified.

And yet, voices across the political spectrum, including many on the left, have described this as a "just war." One longtime advocate of peace, Richard Falk, wrote in *The Nation* that this is "the first truly just war since World War II." Robert Kuttner, another consistent supporter of social jus-tice, declared in *The American Prospect* that only people on the extreme left could believe this is not a just war.

Howard Zinn, "A Just Cause, Not a Just War," *Progressive*, vol. 65, December 2001. Copyright
© 2001 by The Progressive, Inc. Reproduced by permission of The Progressive, 409 East Main
Street, Madison, WI 53703, www.progressive.org.

I have puzzled over this. How can a war be truly just when it involves the daily killing of civilians, when it causes hundreds of thousands of men, women, and children to leave their homes to escape the bombs, when it may not find those who planned the September 11 attacks, and when it will multiply the ranks of people who are angry enough at this country to become terrorists themselves?

This war amounts to a gross violation of human rights, and it will produce the exact opposite of what is wanted: It will not end terrorism; it will proliferate terrorism.

I believe that the progressive supporters of the war have confused a "just cause" with a "just war." There are unjust causes, such as the attempt of the United States to establish its power in Vietnam, or to dominate Panama or Grenada, or to subvert the government of Nicaragua. And a cause may be just—getting North Korea to withdraw from South Korea, getting Saddam Hussein to withdraw from Kuwait, or ending terrorism—but it does not follow that going to war on behalf of that cause, with the inevitable mayhem that follows, is just.

A war waged against innocents

The stories of the effects of our bombing are beginning to come through, in bits and pieces. Just eighteen days into the bombing, *The New York Times* reported: "American forces have mistakenly hit a residential area in Kabul." Twice, U.S. planes bombed Red Cross warehouses, and a Red Cross spokesman said: "Now we've got 55,000 people without that food or blankets, with nothing at all."

An Afghan elementary schoolteacher told a *Washington Post* reporter at the Pakistan border: "When the bombs fell near my house and my babies started crying, I had no choice but to run away."

A cause may be just . . . but it does not follow that going to war on behalf of that cause, with the inevitable mayhem that follows, is just.

A *New York Times* report: "The Pentagon acknowledged that a Navy F/A-18 dropped a 1,000-pound bomb on Sunday near what officials called a center for the elderly. . . . The United Nations said the building was a military hospital. . . . Several hours later, a Navy F-14 dropped two 500-pound bombs on a residential area northwest of Kabul." A U.N. official told a *New York Times* reporter that an American bombing raid on the city of Herat had used cluster bombs, which spread deadly "bomblets" over an area of twenty football fields. This, the *Times* reporter wrote, "was the latest of a growing number of accounts of American bombs going astray and causing civilian casualties."

An Associated Press (A.P.) reporter was brought to Karam, a small mountain village hit by American bombs, and saw houses reduced to rubble. "In the hospital in Jalalabad, twenty-five miles to the east, doctors treated what they said were twenty-three victims of bombing at Karam, one a child barely two months old, swathed in bloody bandages," according to the account. "Another child, neighbors said, was in the hospital because the bombing raid had killed her entire family. At least eighteen fresh graves were scattered around the village."

The city of Kandahar, attacked for seventeen straight days, was reported to be a ghost town, with more than half of its 500,000 people fleeing the bombs. The city's electrical grid had been knocked out. The city was deprived of water, since the electrical pumps could not operate. A sixty-year-old farmer told the A.P. reporter, "We left in fear of our lives. Every day and every night, we hear the roaring and roaring of planes, we see the smoke, the fire. . . . I curse them both—the Taliban and America."

A *New York Times* report from Pakistan two weeks into the bombing campaign told of wounded civilians coming across the border. "Every half-hour or so throughout the day, someone was brought across on a stretcher. . . . Most were bomb victims, missing limbs or punctured by shrapnel. . . . A young boy, his head and one leg wrapped in bloodied bandages, clung to his father's back as the old man trudged back to Afghanistan."

That was only a few weeks into the bombing, and the result had already been to frighten hundreds of thousands of Afghans into abandoning their homes and taking to the dangerous, mine-strewn roads. The "war against terrorism" has become a war against innocent men, women, and children, who are in no way responsible for the terrorist attack on New York.

And yet there are those who say this is a "just war."

"Collateral damage" is murder

Terrorism and war have something in common. They both involve the killing of innocent people to achieve what the killers believe is a good end. I can see an immediate objection to this equation: They (the terrorists) deliberately kill innocent people; we (the war makers) aim at "military targets," and civilians are killed by accident, as "collateral damage."

Is it really an accident when civilians die under our bombs? Even if you grant that the intention is not to kill civilians, if they nevertheless become victims, again and again and again, can that be called an accident? If the deaths of civilians are inevitable in bombing, it may not be deliberate, but it is not an accident, and the bombers cannot be considered innocent. They are committing murder as surely as are the terrorists.

The absurdity of claiming innocence in such cases becomes apparent when the death tolls from "collateral damage" reach figures far greater than the lists of the dead from even the most awful act of terrorism. Thus, the "collateral damage" in the Gulf War caused more people to die—hundreds of thousands, if you include the victims of our sanctions policy—than the very deliberate terrorist attack of September 11. The total of those who have died in Israel from Palestinian terrorist bombs is somewhere under 1,000. The number of dead from "collateral damage" in the bombing of Beirut during Israel's invasion of Lebanon in 1982 was roughly 6,000.

We must not match the death lists—it is an ugly exercise—as if one atrocity is worse than another. No killing of innocents, whether deliberate or "accidental," can be justified. My argument is that when children die at the hands of terrorists, or—whether intended or not—as a result of bombs dropped from airplanes, terrorism and war become equally unpardonable.

Let's talk about "military targets." The phrase is so loose that President Truman, after the nuclear bomb obliterated the population of Hiroshima, could say: "The world will note that the first atomic bomb was dropped on Hiroshima, a military base. That was because we wished in this first attack to avoid, insofar as possible, the killing of civilians."

What we are hearing now from our political leaders is, "We are targeting military objectives. We are trying to avoid killing civilians. But that will happen, and we regret it." Shall the American people take moral comfort from the thought that we are bombing only "military targets"?

Is it really an accident when civilians die under our bombs? . . . [The bombers] are committing murder as surely as are the terrorists.

The reality is that the term "military" covers all sorts of targets that include civilian populations. When our bombers deliberately destroy, as they did in the war against Iraq, the electrical infrastructure, thus making water purification and sewage treatment plants inoperable and leading to epidemic waterborne diseases, the deaths of children and other civilians cannot be called accidental.

Recall that in the midst of the Gulf War, the U.S. military bombed an air raid shelter, killing 400 to 500 men, women, and children who were huddled to escape bombs. The claim was that it was a military target, housing a communications center, but reporters going through the ruins immediately afterward said there was no sign of anything like that.

I suggest that the history of bombing—and no one has bombed more than this nation—is a history of endless atrocities, all calmly explained by deceptive and deadly language like "accident," "military targets," and "collateral damage."

Indeed, in both World War II and in Vietnam, the historical record shows that there was a deliberate decision to target civilians in order to destroy the morale of the enemy—hence the firebombing of Dresden, Hamburg, Tokyo, the B-52s over Hanoi, the jet bombers over peaceful villages in the Vietnam countryside. When some argue that we can engage in "limited military action" without "an excessive use of force," they are ignoring the history of bombing. The momentum of war rides roughshod over limits.

The moral equation in Afghanistan is clear. Civilian casualties are certain. The outcome is uncertain. No one knows what this bombing will accomplish whether it will lead to the capture of Osama Bin Laden (perhaps), or the end of the Taliban (possibly), or a democratic Afghanistan (very unlikely), or an end to terrorism (almost certainly not).

And meanwhile, we are terrorizing the population (not the terrorists, they are not easily terrorized). Hundreds of thousands are packing their belongings and their children onto carts and leaving their homes to make dangerous journeys to places they think might be more safe.

Not one human life should be expended in this reckless violence called a "war against terrorism."

Rejecting war

We might examine the idea of pacifism in the light of what is going on right now. I have never used the word "pacifist" to describe myself, because it suggests something absolute, and I am suspicious of absolutes. I want to leave openings for unpredictable possibilities. There might be situations (and even such strong pacifists as Gandhi and Martin Luther King believed this) when a small, focused act of violence against a monstrous, immediate evil would be justified.

In war, however, the proportion of means to ends is very, very different. War, by its nature, is unfocused, indiscriminate, and especially in our time when the technology is so murderous, inevitably involves the deaths of large numbers of people and the suffering of even more. Even in the "small wars" (Iran vs. Iraq, the Nigerian war, the Afghan war), a million people die. Even in a "tiny" war like the one we waged in Panama, a thousand or more die.

Scott Simon of NPR wrote a commentary in *The Wall Street Journal* on October 11, 2001, entitled, "Even Pacifists Must Support This War." He tried to use the pacifist acceptance of self-defense, which approves a focused resistance to an immediate attacker, to justify this war, which he claims is "self-defense." But the term "self-defense" does not apply when you drop bombs all over a country and kill lots of people other than your attacker. And it doesn't apply when there is no likelihood that it will achieve its desired end.

Pacifism, which I define as a rejection of war, rests on a very powerful logic. In war, the means—indiscriminate killing—are immediate and certain; the ends, however desirable, are distant and uncertain.

Pacifism does not mean "appeasement." That word is often hurled at those who condemn the present war on Afghanistan, and it is accompanied by references to [former British prime ministers Winston] Churchill [and Neville] Chamberlain, [and the] Munich [agreement, which seemed to absolve the British from declaring war against Germany during World War II]. World War II analogies are conveniently summoned forth when there is a need to justify a war, however irrelevant to a particular situation. At the suggestion that we withdraw from Vietnam, or not make war on Iraq, the word "appeasement" was bandied about. The glow of the "good war" has repeatedly been used to obscure the nature of all the bad wars we have fought since 1945.

Not one human life should be expended in this reckless violence called a "war against terrorism."

Let's examine that analogy. Czechoslovakia was handed to the voracious Adolf Hitler to "appease" him. Germany was an aggressive nation expanding its power, and to help it in its expansion was not wise. But today we do not face an expansionist power that demands to be appeased. We ourselves are the expansionist power—troops in Saudi Arabia, bombings of Iraq, military bases all over the world, naval vessels on every sea—and that, along with Israel's expansion into the West Bank and Gaza Strip, has aroused anger.

It was wrong to give up Czechoslovakia to appease Hitler. It is not wrong to withdraw our military from the Middle East, or for Israel to withdraw from the occupied territories, because there is no right to be there. That is not appeasement. That is justice.

Opposing the bombing of Afghanistan does not constitute "giving in to terrorism" or "appeasement." It asks that other means be found than war to solve the problems that confront us. King and Gandhi both believed in action—nonviolent direct action, which is more powerful and certainly more morally defensible than war.

To reject war is not to "turn the other cheek," as pacifism has been caricatured. It is, in the present instance, to act in ways that do not imitate the terrorists.

Let us pull back from being a military superpower, and become a humanitarian superpower.

The United States could have treated the September 11 attack as a horrific criminal act that calls for apprehending the culprits, using every device of intelligence and investigation possible. It could have gone to the United Nations to enlist the aid of other countries in the pursuit and apprehension of the terrorists.

There was also the avenue of negotiations. (And let's not hear: "What? Negotiate with those monsters?" The United States negotiated with—indeed, brought into power and kept in power—some of the most monstrous governments in the world.) Before George W. Bush ordered in the bombers, the Taliban offered to put bin Laden on trial. This was ignored. After ten days of air attacks, when the Taliban called for a halt to the bombing and said they would be willing to talk about handing bin Laden to a third country for trial, the headline the next day in *The New York Times* read: "President Rejects Offer by Taliban for Negotiations," and Bush was quoted as saying: "When I said no negotiations, I meant no negotiations."

That is the behavior of someone hellbent on war. There were similar rejections of negotiating possibilities at the start of the Korean War, the war in Vietnam, the Gulf War, and the bombing of Yugoslavia. The result was an immense loss of life and incalculable human suffering.

International police work and negotiations were—still are—alternatives to war. But let's not deceive ourselves; even if we succeeded in apprehending bin Laden or, as is unlikely, destroying the entire Al Qaeda [terrorist] network, that would not end the threat of terrorism, which has potential recruits far beyond Al Qaeda.

Humanitarian solutions

To get at the roots of terrorism is complicated. Dropping bombs is simple. It is an old response to what everyone acknowledges is a very new situation. At the core of unspeakable and unjustifiable acts of terrorism are justified grievances felt by millions of people who would not themselves engage in terrorism but from whose ranks terrorists spring.

Those grievances are of two kinds: the existence of profound misery—hunger, illness—in much of the world, contrasted to the wealth and luxury of the West, especially the United States; and the presence of American military power everywhere in the world, propping up oppressive regimes and repeatedly intervening with force to maintain U.S. hegemony.

This suggests actions that not only deal with the long-term problem of terrorism but are in themselves just.

Instead of using two planes a day to drop food on Afghanistan and 100 planes to drop bombs (which have been making it difficult for the trucks of the international agencies to bring in food), use 102 planes to bring food.

Take the money allocated for our huge military machine and use it to combat starvation and disease around the world. One-third of our military budget would annually provide clean water and sanitation facilities for the billion people in the world who have none.

Withdraw troops from Saudi Arabia, because their presence near the holy shrines of Mecca and Medina angers not just bin Laden (we need not care about angering him) but huge numbers of Arabs who are not terrorists.

Stop the cruel sanctions on Iraq, which are killing more than a thousand children every week without doing anything to weaken Saddam Hussein's tyrannical hold over the country.

Insist that Israel withdraw from the occupied territories, something that many Israelis also think is right, and which will make Israel more secure than it is now.

In short, let us pull back from being a military superpower, and become a humanitarian superpower.

Let us be a more modest nation. We will then be more secure. The modest nations of the world don't face the threat of terrorism.

Such a fundamental change in foreign policy is hardly to be expected. It would threaten too many interests: the power of political leaders, the ambitions of the military, the corporations that profit from the nation's enormous military commitments.

Change will come, as at other times in our history, only when American citizens—becoming better informed, having second thoughts after the first instinctive support for official policy—demand it. That change in citizen opinion, especially if it coincides with a pragmatic decision by the government that its violence isn't working, could bring about a retreat from the military solution.

It might also be a first step in the rethinking of our nation's role in the world. Such a rethinking contains the promise, for Americans, of genuine security, and for people elsewhere, the beginning of hope.

5

The United States Must Commit to an Ongoing War Against Terrorism

Alan W. Dowd

Alan W. Dowd is a freelance writer whose work has appeared in World & I, Policy Review, *the* Washington Times, *and other publications.*

Just as it took the Japanese bombing of Pearl Harbor during World War II to awaken the United States to the dangers of totalitarianism, it took the September 11, 2001, terrorist attacks for America to truly realize the dangers of global terrorism. But the war on terrorism is more akin to the Cold War than to World War II. As President George W. Bush has repeatedly emphasized, America's war on terrorism will not consist of a single victory, but rather a long series of victories. For America to eliminate global terrorism, it must commit to an extended and costly fight. Increased military actions and spending, renewed intelligence-gathering efforts, and international alliances will all be part of the effort. America's commitment must be firm, because like America's fights against totalitarianism and communism, the war on terrorism is a war to save civilization itself.

"I have lived through a period when one looked forward, as we do now, with anxiety and uncertainty to what would happen in the future," British prime minister Winston Churchill sighed in February 1934, reflecting on the Great War [World War I] and contemplating an even greater war. "Suddenly something did happen—tremendous, swift, overpowering, irresistible." Sixty-eight winters later, with the carnage of [the September 11, 2001, terrorist attacks on America] behind us and the chaos of a strange new war ahead of us, we can relate well to Churchill's feelings of uncertainty and angst.

After being saturated with news and images about the attacks on the World Trade Center and Pentagon, our information-hungry society has been left with the very opposite when it comes to the early counterstrikes of this war on terror. And we can expect more of the same as the war progresses. As President George W. Bush blandly explained in a letter to Congress, "It is not possible to predict the scope and duration of these deployments [or] the actions necessary to counter the terrorist threat to the United States." His advisers and war cabinet talk of an invisible, unconventional war. Echoing the president, Defense Secretary Donald Rumsfeld sprinkles his speeches with words like "shadowy . . . nuanced . . . subtle." In his own words, the battle plan crafted for the war on terror is "distinctly different from prior efforts."

Of course, we didn't need to be told this war would be different. That much was clear at precisely 8:48 A.M. on September 11, when the first of four airliners became a guided missile and slammed into the World Trade Center's north tower. But if the methods and tactics of this war are different, the objectives are not. This first war of the twenty-first century, like the great wars of the twentieth century, is a battle for civilization itself. And as before, the United States is reluctantly marching to the front.

What is civilization?

It may be helpful to define what civilization is and what it is not before considering how it has been defended over the last hundred years. Indeed, one person's civilization is another's Philistia. (Of course, even the Philistines [residents of Philistia, who were thought to lack artistic and cultural values] achieved a kind of civilization, which emphasizes my point.)

Contrary to popular opinion, civilization is not necessarily found where there is Bach or Rembrandt, running water or power grids, interstate highways or Internet access. These things and others may be the byproducts of civilization, but they are not the signs of civilization. Nor is their absence necessarily an indicator of barbarism. Civilization is at once much more and much less than the trappings of modernity. It is the intangible, not the material, that separates the civilized world from the barbaric. It is what motivates a culture or society or group that determines whether it is a part of civilization or an enemy of civilization. Consider the authors of September 11, for example. They possessed vast stores of creativity, exhibited remarkable sophistication, mastered the tools of civilization and modernity, and yet conceived and executed an act of unthinkable barbarism. To paraphrase Churchill's assessment of the Nazis, the men who carried out the homicidal hijackings and suicidal mass murders of September 11 spliced togther "the latest refinements of science [with] the cruelties of the Stone Age."

Some of them were educated at the great institutions of higher learning in Europe and America. They were polyglots and world travelers, speaking Arabic, German, and English, while living in Hamburg and Cairo and Boston. They had all the trappings of wealth, relied on computers and cell phones, and were trained to fly the most modern of jet aircraft, but they were anything but civilized. Thousands of their kind still roam the earth. No matter how many Qur'anic suras they twist to justify their crimes or salve their consciences, these men are as barbaric as Attila. And Islam isn't any more responsible for spawning them than Russian Orthodoxy is to blame for Joseph Stalin. (The second Soviet dictator was studying to be an Orthodox monk in Tbilisi when he rechanneled his religious fervor from hagiography to Vladimir Lenin worship.) The Islamic world, which helped preserve and protect the discoveries of Greek antiquity, has contributed much to civilization in its own right, from science to government administration to philosophy. As the president said, the men who bankrolled and hatched the attacks of September 11 "are traitors to their own faith [and] blaspheme the name of Allah."

It is not possible to predict the scope and duration of . . . the actions necessary to counter the terrorist threat to the United States.

Like Stalin and Hitler, they were incubated in a crevice of rage and lies. We caught a glimpse of that crevice after the attacks of September 11, and it painted a graphic picture of what civilization is and what it is not. Civilization strives to protect the weak, the unarmed, the innocent. Its enemies target them. Civilization weeps when innocents are slaughtered; its enemies dance in the street. Civilization is sickened by the hecatomb of September 11; its enemies are emboldened by it. Civilization teaches that war is an evil to be avoided; its enemies, that war is a divine commandment to be followed. Civilization borrows from the best of every culture it encounters, creating something new and better than before the encounter. Its enemies lack the self-confidence to take such a risk. Civilization glories in difference and diversity; its enemies, in sameness and submission, conformity and control.

And it has always been this way. When pharaoh denied Moses' request for a day of worship, it was a battle between civilization and barbarism. But ironically, it wasn't pharaoh, with his modern armies, sprawling metropolises, and gleaming architecture, who represented civilization. It was Moses, with little more than a splintery cane and a profound idea: Let people choose their own god and worship it in their own way.

The battle has taken countless forms since then, but at its core it always has to do with control and power, and how they are used. To his credit, the president grasps this truth: "Its goal," Bush said of [terrorist Osama] bin Laden's al Qaeda terror syndicate, "is remaking the world and imposing its radical beliefs on people everywhere." That is why, in Bush's view, America must rally the civilized world to "the destruction and defeat of the global terror network."

Four battles, one war

Even so, many scoff when "civilization" and "America" are used in the same sentence. French statesman Georges Clemenceau's sneering assessment of his wartime ally still captures what many believe on both sides of the Atlantic and Pacific: "America is the only nation in history which miraculously has gone directly from barbarism to degeneration without the usual interval of civilization."

Moreover, the scoffers argue, America has played a part in the ageless battle between civilization and darkness for only a couple of centuries—barely the blink of an eye in the millennia of recorded history—and it has been in the lead role for just eighty of those years. In those eight decades, civilization has faced perhaps its sternest tests and darkest hours. Often, it was the United States that held back the curtain.

Indeed, who was left to rescue the Old World from the war it unleashed in 1914—a war that, it pays to recall, began with an act of terror? Regardless of what the kings and princes of Europe thought, America saw its entry into the Great War as nothing less than an effort to save Europe from itself—and civilization from Europe. In fact, during his war address, President Woodrow Wilson argued that "civilization itself" was teetering in the balance. He wasn't accused of hyperbole and for good reason. As Churchill would later write, it was during the Great War that "all the horrors of all the ages were brought together." Even after a century of mass murder, the costs remain staggering: a million Brits, 1.7 million Frenchmen, 1.8 million Germans, perhaps 2 million Russians, and some 10 million noncombatants. Perhaps Clemenceau's swipe would have been better directed at his side of the Atlantic.

Gasping at what Europe had wrought, Wilson called the cataclysm "the most terrible and disastrous of all wars." He howled against submarine warfare as "a challenge to all mankind . . . a war against all nations." After describing submarine attacks against hospital and relief ships, he even conceded that he was "unable to believe that such things would be done by any government." Wilson vowed to make the world "safe for democracy . . . to vindicate the principles of peace and justice"—principles that, from his vantage point, only America understood.

Like Wilson and Truman, Bush has framed the war [on terrorism] as a struggle for civilization itself.

Less than a quarter-century later, Franklin D. Roosevelt would echo Wilson's shock at the behavior of another faraway empire [during World War II]. For Roosevelt and his generation, it was imperial Japan. "The United States," he thundered, "was at peace with that nation and, at the solicitation of Japan, was still in conversation with its government," even as the bombs began to fall on Oahu [during the attack on Pearl Harbor]. To Roosevelt, the sneak attack was as dastardly as the kaiser's submarine warfare a generation earlier. And for its day, Japan's undeclared, unannounced war on America was arguably as shocking as the twin assaults of September 11. "Always we will remember the character of this onslaught against us," he concluded. "We will not only defend ourselves to the uttermost, but will make very certain that this form of treachery shall never endanger us again."

When Churchill heard the news of Japan's attack, he is said to have responded not with dread but relief. For the first time in months, he later wrote, "I went to bed and slept the sleep of the saved and thankful." Churchill knew what Clemenceau was too arrogant to admit: America was civilization's best hope. "With her left hand," he marveled in the months following that first day of infamy, "America was leading the advance of the conquering Allied armies into the heart of Germany, and with her right, on the other side of the globe, she was irresistibly and swiftly breaking up the power of Japan."

Like his wartime predecessors, Harry Truman would rally the nation yet again to civilization's defense. His 1947 address to Congress, which described the deteriorating state of affairs in Greece, Turkey, and all across Europe, amounted to a declaration of war—a conflict perhaps similar to the one the United States entered September 11, if only in its strangeness and newness. For the plainspeaking Truman, this still-nameless war was nothing more than an extension of World War II, which America fought so that "we and other nations [would] be able to work out a way of life free from coercion." According to Truman, that goal could not be realized unless the United States was "willing to help free peoples maintain their free institutions and their national integrity." Calling on Congress to send a staggering $400 million to Greece and Turkey, Truman explained that the next battle for civilization would be fought and won not just with weapons but with money—lots of money. "We are the only country able to provide that help," he warned. "Should we fail to aid Greece and Turkey in this fateful hour, the effect will be far reaching to the West and to the East."

Truman went on to sketch the grim outlines of a postwar world without America in the lead: "terror and oppression" in Europe, "disorder . . . throughout the Middle East," the peace of the entire world at risk, and the welfare of America itself endangered. With Moscow's conquest of Eastern Europe in full view, Congress agreed. And so began the Cold War. Over the next four decades, the United States would sacrifice one hundred thousand lives, build and man more than six hundred overseas bases, and spend some $5 trillion to wage and win the last war of the twentieth century.

It wasn't French treatises, Italian frescoes, or Austrian concertos that preserved civilization during the terrors of the twentieth century—it was blood and bullets. The same holds true today. As historian John Keegan argues, in his *History of Warfare*, "All civilizations owe their origins to the warrior." And since America alone stood as the last line of defense between civilization and a second Dark Age, in a very real sense modern civilization owes its continued existence to the United States, civilization's reluctant but tenacious warrior.

The American military must now match the enemy's audacity, while the American people imitate its patience.

That brings us to what President George W. Bush calls "the first war of the twenty-first century," the war on terror. Like Wilson and Truman, Bush has framed the war as a struggle for civilization itself. "This is the world's fight," he explained during his own war address to Congress. "This is civilization's fight." Like Roosevelt, Bush has allowed his simmering rage to boil over with words of shock and revulsion, calling the masterminds of September 11 murderous, barbaric, and evil, while promising to defeat and destroy them. "We will not tire, we will not falter, and we will not fail," he intoned, as if reading from a decades-old script handed down from Wilson to Roosevelt to Truman. "We have found our mission and our moment," he added, standing where those others rallied a hermit republic to civilization's rescue: "The advance of human freedom . . . now depends on us."

Although every corner of the globe is within terrorism's reach—the horrors of September 11 make that clear—perhaps for the first time in the history of terror, the carriers and breeding grounds of this scourge are finally within reach of justice and punishment. That's because, as Bush explained in his address to Congress, the world profoundly and dramatically changed on September 11. According to Bush, friend and foe alike now "understand that if this terror goes unpunished, their own cities, their own citizens may be next."

Indeed, it was as if America's fair-weather friends and critics awoke on September 11 to catch a glimpse of their wildest dreams come true—an America shaken, bloodied, humbled, and ready to retreat. And what they saw frightened them and forced them to reevaluate their place in the world. For others, the day of terror silenced decades of criticism directed at Tel Aviv [Israel, the target of frequent Palestinian terrorist attacks]. Finally, they saw the true nature of the enemy Israel had battled for a half-century. In that moment, perhaps they realized, like John F. Kennedy at the Berlin Wall, that the civilized world must stand together: We are all Israelis; we are all New Yorkers.

Warning signs

If the rhetoric of this new war echoes that of other wars, so does America's prewar obliviousness to the likelihood of war. The carnage of September 11 is only an exclamation point to a half-century of terror—much of which went unpunished and all of which led inexorably, if indirectly, to that awful Tuesday morning. Only now has the battle been joined. Indeed, the terrorists have been waging this war far longer than Americans care to admit.

Terrorism became part of life in Europe thirty years ago, and in the Middle East even earlier. In fact, Michael Walzer argues in his book *Just and Unjust Wars* that terrorism emerged as an identifiable strategy for revolutionary groups soon after World War II. British historian Niall Ferguson adds, "Since 1968, there have been 500 hijackings around the world and more than 4,000 recorded terrorist bombings." And as Paul Johnson writes in his landmark survey of the twentieth century, *Modern Times*, by 1980 there were some 1,700 international terrorist incidents annually. Even then, the terrorists didn't limit their attacks to the helpless people and politicians of Belfast, Cairo, or New Delhi. They imprisoned American civilians in Tehran, kidnapped American emissaries in the Middle East, and bombed American servicemen in Berlin and Beirut. By the mid-1980s, terrorism had claimed well over 250 American lives.

In short, we should have seen this coming. Step by step, the terrorists have been creeping closer and growing bolder. However, it wasn't until the 1990s that global terrorists were able to strike American targets at will—both at home and abroad. In 1993, the terrorists threw their first blows at the World Trade Center, killing 6 Americans, injuring 1,000, and shattering the peace of mind of millions. Later that year, Saudi expatriate

Osama bin Laden first made news by taking credit for the ambush in Mogadishu, which claimed 17 U.S. soldiers. In 1996, a truck bomb that exploded outside the U.S. military's Khobar Towers in Saudi Arabia claimed 19 airmen and injured 200 others. In 1998, bin Laden's network bombed a pair of American embassies in East Africa, murdering 224 civilians, injuring more than 5,000, and foreshadowing the group's capacity to plan and execute coordinated attacks. And in October 2000, terrorists used a rubber boat to blast a hole in the USS *Cole*, killing 17 sailors.

All of this occurred against a bloody backdrop of global terrorism. In fact, the year 2000 saw an 8 percent increase in terrorist attacks worldwide. According to the State Department, 21,000 people were killed or maimed by organized acts of terror between 1995 and 2000. The numbers for 2001 are not yet tallied, but we know this much: More than 6,000 people, almost all of them civilians, were added to terrorism's death toll on a single day of slow-motion horror in September.

Democracies and dinosaurs

Rather than heeding all the warnings—rather than taking the war to the terrorists and their sponsors before the unthinkable came upon our homeland—we sleepwalked through a decade, hoping that stern words and pinpricks would be enough. In this way, we were no different than countless other democracies, some of them no longer on the face of the earth, that waited too long to awake.

Why it takes a December 7 [1941, Pearl Harbor] or September 11 for America to answer civilization's distress call could be the subject of a book. The eminent American diplomat George Kennan reasoned that such complacency is just one of the many undesirable by products of democracy. As he explained in the early hours of the Cold War, a democracy is something like a dinosaur blithely frolicking in the mud: "He pays little attention to his environment; he is slow to wrath—in fact, you practically have to whack his tail off to make him aware that his interests are being disturbed," Kennan observed. "But once he grasps this, he lays about him with such blind determination that he not only destroys his adversary but largely wrecks his native habitat." This seems especially true of the American democracy.

Viewing America through the distorted and grimy prism of our own popular culture, our adversaries don't understand that beneath the soft outer edges of democracy there exist muscle and bone that can unleash an unspeakable fury. In this new war, those muscles will be flexed—and strained—like they haven't been in sixty years. America clearly has the capacity to handle the strain: Any nation that can withstand the body blows of September 11 has a vast reservoir of resilience. What remains to be seen is whether the country has the audacity and patience for the war on terror. The latter-day kamikazes who attacked the World Trade Center and the Pentagon had plenty of both. Planning and preparing for the attacks may have taken three to five years. The operation itself was so audacious that no one in Washington had even considered it as a possibility—until 8:48 A.M. on September 11.

The American military must now match the enemy's audacity, while the American people imitate his patience. The latter will be far more difficult. After all, America is the land of fast food, FedEx, and fax machines. Patience has never been a virtue for Americans. A quarter-century of push-button, nearly bloodless warfare has not helped to prepare us for what lies ahead. And what lies ahead of us, in front of us, and all around us is a war for which we are ill-prepared.

The early blows of our vengeance may be swift, but victory will not be.

This, too, was predictable. Almost fifteen years ago, with the Cold War thawing into a new era of peace, we shoved defense spending into a free fall. It spiraled from 6.1 percent of GDP in 1987 to 2.9 percent in 2000, leading some observers to make ominous comparisons to the post–World War I military drawdown. In 1919, the country invested 16 percent of GDP in national defense. On the eve of war in 1937, as Germany spent 23.5 percent and Japan 28.2 percent of GDP to expand their arsenals, the United States devoted a paltry 1.5 percent to defense. That was enough to protect America—or better said, to maintain the illusion of protection—until December 7, 1941. Sudden death and destruction have a way of shattering such illusions.

Churchill's lament as war clouds gathered over Europe is now ours: "When I think of the immense combinations and resources which have been neglected or squandered," he gasped, "I cannot believe that a parallel exists in the whole of history." It does now, as Washington and New York are forever linked to London by a bond of terror and blood.

Shadows and twilight

But all is not lost. As William Ewart Gladstone, another of Britain's redoubtable prime ministers, observed a half-century before World War II, "The resources of civilization are not yet exhausted." They won't be as long as there are people willing to fight and bleed for civilization. Almost 120,000 Americans died in the eighteen months of slaughter between Wilson's war address and the armistice. Four bloody years passed before America made good on FDR's promise "to win through to absolute victory," before the shock and infamy of Pearl Harbor turned into the fury of Midway, Dresden, Normandy, and Hiroshima. It would take two generations of proxy wars and nuclear stalemate before America smothered Soviet communism.

As the civilized world begins to strike back at terrorism, there is much to be learned from those wars and others. The war on terror will borrow from all of them and, in so doing, will resemble none of them. As President Bush cautioned, "Victory against terrorism will not take place in a single battle, but in a series of decisive actions against terrorist organizations and those who harbor and sponsor them." Even at this moment, American troops are waging these pitched battles, throwing covert and overt counterpunches at a vast global network of terror. They are fighting in the air, at sea, on land, in cyberspace, close to home, and far away. Yet we have only seen the faintest outlines of this strange new war.

The early blows of our vengeance may be swift, but victory will not be. Indeed, it cannot be, if this war is to achieve what most Americans demand—the end to terrorism itself. To realize that goal, the war will require a little of everything from the Pentagon: surgical strikes like the miniwars against Belgrade and Baghdad, and sustained bombing campaigns that call to mind the latter days of Vietnam. There will be secret assaults known only to America's shadow warriors and their targets; draining tests of will that recall the long twilight struggle between communism and freedom; modern-day Marshall Plans to prop up shaky allies; multiagency raids that borrow from the war on drugs; mundane detective work at home and methodical campaigns against terror's financial infrastructure abroad; awkward allied endeavors that invoke memories of Kosovo and Sicily; plans to reorder the world that echo Versailles; failures that awaken the ghosts of Desert One and Mogadishu; and, very likely, moments of horror that parallel or even eclipse September 11.

That possibility alone should serve as a grim reminder that there are vast differences between yesterday's battles for civilization and today's. The enemy that sunk the *Lusitania*, torpedoed Pearl Harbor, and blockaded Berlin had the courage to show his face. Although the nation's sons were bloodied in those battles, the nation itself was untouched.

We enjoy neither the pretense of a conventional war nor the illusion of invulnerability today. The first was ripped away from us when those three jets, symbols of our independence and freedom and modernity, turned against our cities. The other disappeared moments later, in a flash of flame and a shower of shrapnel. In all likelihood, we may never enjoy the thrill and satisfaction of victory either. Indeed, we may not know this war is over until years after the final shots are fired, when we emerge, Lazaruslike, from the tombs and bunkers of our post–September 11 world to breathe the air and feel the sun once again.

When that moment comes, we should treasure it—such moments are rare and all too brief in the history of mankind. We should not delude ourselves yet again into believing that civilization's enemies have been vanquished. Civilization will always have enemies. If we grow complacent, they will strike again—as suddenly and swiftly as they did on September 11, 2001.

6

An Unconstrained War Against Terrorism Would Be Unethical and Unconstitutional

William Norman Grigg

William Norman Grigg is senior editor of the New American, *a conservative monthly magazine.*

The September 11, 2001, terrorist attacks on America justified a military response, but the ongoing "war on terrorism" fails several critical moral and constitutional tests. Having achieved a limited victory in Afghanistan by ousting the Taliban (but failing to capture terrorist Osama bin Laden, who is suspected of masterminding the September 11 attacks), President George W. Bush has become intent on committing America to a state of perpetual war. However, the president does not have the constitutional authority to declare war—only Congress does. Moreover, an endless war on terrorism would cost countless lives and is, therefore, immoral. Congress should reclaim its constitutional role, put an end to the proposed perpetual war on terrorism, and demand that the U.S. military be used for national defense rather than foreign intervention.

"Our war on terror is well begun, but it is only begun," declared President George W. Bush in his January 29th, 2002, State of the Union address. "This campaign may not be finished on our watch—yet it must and it will be waged on our watch." While the president's display of resolution drew enthusiastic bipartisan applause, it provoked a more ambivalent response from those who recall that throughout history, war has been regarded as a curse—a pitiless scourge that depletes national wealth, constricts individual freedom, and devours the lives of the bravest men.

James Madison observed in 1795, "Of all the enemies to public liberty, war is, perhaps, the most to be dreaded, because it comprises and de-

William Norman Grigg, "How Best to Achieve Justice?: A Military Response to the Black Tuesday Atrocity Was Necessary, but the Ongoing 'War on Terrorism' Fails Several Critical Moral and Constitutional Tests," *New American*, vol. 18, February 25, 2002, p. 24. Copyright © 2002 by *New American*. Reproduced by permission.

velops the germ of every other. War is the parent of armies; from these proceed debts and taxes; and armies, and debts, and taxes are the known instruments for bringing the many under the domination of the few. . . . No nation could preserve its freedom in the midst of continual warfare."

President Bush's address seemed an ironic tribute to the accuracy of Madison's dire warning. Set against the backdrop of a potentially endless war, Mr. Bush's speech outlined vast new expenditures for the military and the new "homeland defense" apparatus, as well as a new "national service" initiative that would accelerate the regimentation of our nation's domestic life. The address also acknowledged that the "war on terror" would require a new round of deficit spending.

Of course, our nation should not remain passive in the face of the Black Tuesday atrocity [the September 11, 2001, terrorist attacks on America]. The blood of our innocent dead cries out for justice—both the eternal justice that God alone can provide, and the temporal variety that our government was intended to pursue. But a righteous cause does not consecrate morally defective means. When measured against the U.S. Constitution and the Christian "Just War" tradition, the ongoing "war on terrorism" must be judged a morally tainted exercise.

Moral tests of war

Although the Just War concept is most strongly identified with the Catholic faith, its principles have been widely accepted throughout Christendom. St. Augustine and St. Thomas Aquinas are regarded as the fathers of the Just War doctrine, and notable scholars of the "law of nations," such as 17th-century Dutch legal commentator Hugo Grotius and 18th-century Swiss jurist Emmerich de Vattel, have also elaborated on the concept. "The just-war tradition is not an algebra that provides custom-made, clear-cut answers under all circumstances," notes Catholic scholar George Weigel. Rather, it is intended "to provide guidance to public authorities on whom the responsibilities of decision-making fall."

Just War theory involves two sets of moral criteria: the *jus ad bello*, or "war decision law"; and *jus in bello*, or "war conduct law." To be regarded as morally sound, a "responsible public authority" must make the decision to go to war. It must be the product of a "right intention," such as "re-establishing justice when offended, repairing an injury, or defending oneself against aggression" observes Monsignor Luigi Civardi. The envisioned war must also be "proportionate"—meaning that the good accomplished by war would be greater than the evil that would result were another alternative pursued. And all other reasonable avenues of redress must be exhausted before a nation resorts to arms.

A morally sound decision to go to war being made, the ensuing campaign is subject to the "war conduct law." This standard deals, once again, with the test of "proportionality," as well as the principle of "discrimination." Dr. Charles Rice, a professor of law at Notre Dame University, explains that "Proportionality relates not only to the war itself (i.e., the whole enterprise must be for a proportionate good), but also to the use of particular tactics or weapons. . . ." Under the principle of "discrimination," Dr. Rice continues, "it can never be justified intentionally to kill innocent noncombatants"—although "it could be morally justified to attack a military target of sufficient importance and urgency even though the attacker knows, but does not intend, that innocent civilians in the vicinity will be killed."

Significantly, the Bush administration has insisted that its conduct of the opening phase of the "war on terrorism"—the bombing campaign against Afghanistan—comports with the Just War doctrine's "war conduct law." Writing in the December 24, 2001, issue of *The Weekly Standard*, Joe Loconte, a religious scholar with the Heritage Foundation, described a meeting at the Pentagon between Defense Secretary Donald Rumsfeld and a group of Catholic, Protestant, Jewish, and Islamic clerics. After reviewing details of the military campaign in Afghanistan, the group concluded that "the United States has waged a war on terrorists while mostly avoiding civilian casualties—which is to say it is fighting a just war with just means." Having attended the meeting, evangelical leader Charles Colson insisted that the military campaign in Afghanistan "would fit the Augustinian-Aquinas play-book perfectly."

Many neutral observers on the ground in Afghanistan, whose access to the battlefield has been unfiltered and much more comprehensive, have come to drastically different conclusions. But the conduct of the war is the subject of [another] article. The present discussion will examine whether the ongoing "war on terrorism" satisfies the first set of Just War criteria, the "war decision law." In our republic, such questions must be examined in light of the assigned powers set forth in the U.S. Constitution.

One man's decision?

"When I called our troops into action," observed the president during his State of the Union address, "I did so with complete confidence in their courage and skill." That the murderous aggression against our country justified a military response is beyond dispute. But was it the president's proper role to commit our nation to a war against Afghanistan?

The Black Tuesday attack was an act of war, and President Bush acted in accord with his constitutional responsibilities by taking steps to protect our nation against further assaults. Before the day was through, however, the president and his advisors had mapped out a lengthy military campaign that could involve military action in 60 countries, beginning with Afghanistan—where terrorist chieftain Osama bin Laden based his operations. "Let's pick them off one at a time" Mr. Bush told his emergency "war cabinet."

Secretary of Defense Donald Rumsfeld informed the president that it would take weeks to organize an effective military campaign. The president had ample time to seek a congressional declaration of war, as the Constitution dictates. Such a declaration would have received nearly unanimous support. President Bush, however, chose a different course.

Early on the morning of September 12th, Bush called British Prime Minister Tony Blair to confer about the possibility of assembling an "international coalition" to carry out the military campaign. "The two leaders agreed it was important to first move quickly on the diplomatic front to capitalize on the international outrage about the terrorist attack," reports the *Washington Post*. "If they got support from NATO and the United Nations, they reasoned, *they would have the legal and political framework to permit a military response afterward."* (Emphasis added.)

The Bush administration acted quickly to obtain the approval of the UN and its regional affiliate, NATO. The North Atlantic Council invoked Article V of the NATO charter, describing the Black Tuesday atrocity as an attack on the entire alliance. And the UN Security Council passed Resolution 1373, a measure drafted by the Bush administration's UN representative to authorize the "war on terrorism."

One gets authorization from a superior, not from a subordinate. In seeking permission to take our nation to war, President Bush was willing to defer to the UN Security Council, but not to Congress.

Nine days after the attack on our country, the president made a dramatic televised address to a joint session of Congress in which he identified the Taliban regime then in control of Afghanistan as a state sponsor of Osama bin Laden's al-Qaeda terrorist network. The Taliban junta, the president declared, "is threatening people everywhere by sponsoring and sheltering and supplying terrorists. By aiding and abetting murder, the Taliban regime is committing murder."

This statement is in harmony with the established principles of the "law of nations," as understood by the Constitution's Framers. By providing shelter and material aid to terrorists within its borders, a government becomes party to any violations of international peace they commit. Accordingly, the president acted properly in presenting an ultimatum to the Taliban regime: "They will hand over the terrorists, or they will share in their fate."

When measured against the U.S. Constitution and the Christian "Just War" tradition, the ongoing "war on terrorism" must be judged a morally tainted exercise.

However, the president failed an important Just War test when the Taliban suggested that it might be willing to surrender bin Laden and his henchmen—if the United States provided evidence of their guilt. While the Taliban's offer might not have been made in good faith, the Just War doctrine required that we make a good faith effort to obtain satisfaction by means other than war. If the Taliban offer proved insincere, then a Just War could be declared and prosecuted to its conclusion.

But the president, in any case, conspicuously declined to request a declaration of war from Congress. Some observers have claimed that since only a scant handful of Muslim states recognized the Taliban junta, it was illegitimate—and thus not a proper target of a declaration of war. But President Bush treated the Taliban as the legitimate governing authority when he demanded its cooperation in arresting and extraditing terrorists. If the Taliban was a suitable subject for a presidential ultimatum, it was just as suitable a target for a congressional declaration of war.

Under the "law of nations" as understood by the Founding Fathers, declarations of war are intended to put both governments and their subjects on notice of impending hostilities. Reflecting the recognized international conventions at the time of the American founding, Emmerich de Vattel pointed out in his definitive work *The Law of Nations* that issuing a declaration of war is a duty owed "to humanity, and especially to the lives and peace of the subjects" of the hostile government. By issuing such a declaration, the aggrieved nation formally notifies "that unjust nation, or its chief, that we are at length going to have recourse to the last remedy, for the purpose of bringing him to reason."

Vattel also emphasized that where "custom has introduced certain formalities in the business" of declaring war, those formalities must be dutifully observed, unless they have been "set . . . aside by a public renunciation." In the case of the United States of America, the "formalities" in question are specifically defined not by custom, but by the Constitution—which has not been amended to relieve the president of his duty to seek a formal declaration from Congress.

Congressional abdication

Prior to the president's September 20, 2001 address, Congress passed a joint resolution authorizing the president "to use all necessary and appropriate force against those nations, organizations, or persons *he determines* planned, authorized, or aided the terrorist attacks on September 11." (Emphasis added.) As commentator Sheldon Richman observes, that resolution was not a declaration of war, but "a grant of Caesarian power." When asked if the president would have to obtain congressional authorization to attack nations other than Afghanistan, Senate Majority Leader Tom Daschle (D-S.D.) replied: "No, he certainly wouldn't have to clear it with us. He's an independent branch of government." Daschle's reply misrepresents the Constitution's division of war powers between the executive and legislative branches. In our constitutional system, the president does not have the privilege of committing our nation to war; only Congress has the power to make that decision.

The description of the president as "commander in chief" of our military describes a function, not an office. In peacetime, this presidential role insures civilian control of our military. But even in wartime, the president exercises his role under a mandate from Congress, and subject to its budgetary and regulatory restraints.

In carrying out the functions of commander in chief, wrote Alexander Hamilton in *The Federalist*, No. 69, the president's authority "would be nominally the same with that of the king of Great Britain, but in substance much inferior to it. It would amount to nothing more than the supreme command and direction of the military and naval forces . . . while that of the British king extends to the raising and regulating of fleets and armies, all which, by the Constitution . . . appertain to the legislature."

In a June 1793 essay written as the infant American republic confronted the prospect of a war with Britain, Hamilton re-emphasized the primacy of Congress' role in committing our nation to war: "It is the province and duty of the Executive to preserve to the Nation the blessings of peace. The Legislature alone can interrupt those blessings, by placing the Nation in a state of War."

Notably, Hamilton was an outspoken proponent of "energy in the executive." But like the other Framers of the Constitution, he insisted that the president should devote his energies to carrying out the constitutionally sound measures passed by Congress—including declarations of war.

War without end?

In a 1798 letter to Thomas Jefferson, James Madison pointed out: "The Constitution supposes, what the history of all governments demonstrates, that the executive is the branch of power most interested in war, and most prone to it. It has accordingly with studied care, vested the question of war in the legislature." Allowing the executive to decide unilaterally "the question of war" would be tantamount to installing a monarchy—and potentially set the stage for "continual warfare," a condition in which liberty cannot long survive.

The Bush administration has eagerly acted upon Congress' open-ended grant of power. In early January 2002, Secretary of State Defense Rumsfeld warned that 15 countries are potential targets of U.S. military strikes. Rumsfeld has also advised that the "war on terror" might last for more than a single lifetime, and Bush administration strategists have reportedly been reviewing contingency plans for a conflict lasting 50 years or more.

By abdicating its constitutional war powers, Congress violated a key tenet of the Just War doctrine. President Bush committed an even more grievous violation by ignoring Congress and deferring to the supposed authority of the UN Security Council to authorize his decision to take our nation to war.

"We are supported by the collective will of the world. . . . [T]he world has come together to fight a new and different war," insisted the president in the White House report *The Global War on Terrorism: The First 100 Days*. In a similar vein, UN Secretary-General Kofi Annan has stated with satisfaction that by presiding over the global "war on terrorism," the world body is providing "collective global defense against a global enemy." By doing so, the UN is rapidly gaining both the power and the pretense of legitimacy it needs to become the seat of a socialist World State.

In our constitutional system, the president does not have the privilege of committing our nation to war; only Congress has the power to make that decision.

In addition, our nation's unwise involvement in a UN-directed "anti-terrorism" coalition has made us allies with some of the world's most notorious terrorist states. Syria, a chief exporter of terrorism, presently sits on the UN Security Council, where it helps preside over the "war on terrorism."

Until the president described it as part of the "axis of evil," Iran was also a member of the UN-directed coalition. Iran is a patron of Osama bin Laden, and a surrogate of Russia—itself a permanent member of the UN Security Council. Communist China, another permanent Security Council member, generously supplied military hardware and assistance to Afghanistan's Taliban junta. And the Northern Alliance, brought to power with the backing of the UN-organized coalition, is a hideous collection of terrorists, drug traffickers, and degenerates that differs from the Taliban only in matters of nuance. How can a "war on terrorism" in which terrorists are our comrades-in-arms be considered just?

The primary stated objective of the war on Afghanistan was to get Osama bin Laden. Yet when bin Laden and his chief lieutenant, Mullah Omar, eluded capture, the coalition declared victory because the Northern Alliance [Afghanistan rebels opposed to the ruling Taliban] had supplanted the Taliban. In addition, the president has warned that tens of thousands of bin Laden's terrorists have fled Afghanistan and pose a continuing threat to our nation. Given all of this, it would appear that the war on Afghanistan fails the test of proportionality.

The costs of perpetual war, as measured in lives, liberties, wealth, and national independence, also appear to violate the Just War principle of proportionality. The same principle requires exploring alternatives to warfare. The only realistic alternative to an interminable "war on terrorism" is to repudiate our present interventionist foreign policy and restore the Founding Fathers' policy of enlightened neutrality.

That policy would dictate non-intervention in the affairs of other nations coupled with maintaining a military geared exclusively toward national defense. It would require that Congress re-claim its constitutional role as the sole body with the power to commit our nation to war. And, most importantly, it would demand that our nation liberate itself from the United Nations—which, far from being the world's "last, best hope for peace," is becoming an engine for perpetual war.

7

A U.S. Invasion
of Iraq Is Justified

Frank J. Gaffney Jr.

Frank J. Gaffney Jr. held senior positions in the Reagan Defense De-partment. He is currently president of the Center for Security Policy in Washington.

Iraqi leader Saddam Hussein is a tyrant responsible for the deaths of thousands of people. Moreover, his regime has developed weapons of mass destruction—including anthrax, nerve gas, and ballistic missiles—that could be used to kill countless more. Iraq has also helped train and finance al Qaeda and other terrorist groups. The United States should not wait for Iraq to use its weapons of mass destruction, or allow them to be used by terror-ists. Rather, the United States should confront this threat and force regime change in Iraq. Diplomatic efforts and economic sanctions have failed, and the time has come to use military force to depose Saddam Hussein.

In February 1998 a group of distinguished security-policy practitioners addressed an open letter to President Bill Clinton under the banner of the Committee for Peace and Security in the Gulf. The signatories were seized with what was even then a pressing problem: the need to remove Saddam Hussein from power.

These experts—many of whom now hold top positions in the Bush administration (including Secretary of Defense Donald Rumsfeld, Deputy Secretary of Defense Paul Wolfowitz, Deputy Secretary of State Richard Armitage, Undersecretaries of State John Bolton and Paula Dobriansky and Undersecretaries of Defense Douglas Feith and Dov Zakheim)—felt compelled to call for regime change in Iraq for reasons that are, if any-thing, still more compelling now:

> Despite [Saddam's] defeat in the [Persian] Gulf War, continu-ing sanctions and the determined effort of U.N. inspectors to fetter out and destroy his weapons of mass destruction, Sad-dam Hussein has been able to develop biological and chemi-

cal munitions. To underscore the threat posed by these deadly devices, [then–Secretary of State Madeleine Albright and then–Secretary of Defense William Cohen] have said that these weapons could be used against our own people. . . .

Iraq's position is unacceptable. While Iraq is not unique in possessing these weapons, it is the only country which has used them—not just against its enemies, but its own people as well. We must assume that Saddam is prepared to use them again. This poses a danger to our friends, our allies and to our nation.

Today, some four years after the last U.N. weapons inspector was compelled to leave Iraq, Saddam not only has active chemical and bio-weapons programs but surely also has resumed the aggressive effort he was making before Operation Desert Storm to acquire atomic and, in due course, thermonuclear arms.

Defectors have revealed that his covert program is so far advanced technologically that the only thing preventing Saddam from having fully functional nuclear weapons is access to sufficient quantities of fissile material. Once he has enriched uranium or plutonium, he would be able at a minimum to build radiological, or "dirty," bombs. It strains credulity that, given his vast oil revenues and the black market that has developed in such material since the collapse of the Soviet empire, this need will go unfulfilled for very long—if it has not already begun to be satisfied.

We now have compelling evidence of Iraq's involvement in international terrorism.

Saddam continues to work as well at building the means of delivering such weapons of mass destruction (WMDs) against targets farther removed than his own people. (The gruesome details of his use of chemical weapons against Kurdish population centers in 1988 recently has been documented by Jeffrey Goldberg in the *New Yorker* magazine.) Fighter aircraft, cruise missiles and ballistic missiles capable of serving this purpose—at least with small payloads of chemical or biological weapons—are in his inventory today. Given the closed nature of Iraq under Saddam's misrule, it is reasonable to expect that this equipment's capability for WMD applications is being secretly modernized with the assistance of the Russian, Chinese and/or North Korean technicians who busily are proliferating WMDs and relevant delivery systems throughout the Middle East and, indeed, the world.

Iraq's support of terrorism

The danger that such weapons might be used by Saddam against the United States is today even more clear than it was when Rumsfeld et al. addressed the topic in 1998. After all, we now have compelling evidence of Iraq's involvement in international terrorism. Iraq expert and best-selling author Laurie Mylroie has argued convincingly that Iraqi intelligence was implicated in the first World Trade Center bombing in 1993.

And there is more compelling evidence tying Mohammed Atta (the terrorist believed to have led the hijackers on the devastating Sept. 11, 2001, attack on the World Trade Center twin towers) to Saddam than there is to Osama bin Laden. (This includes Atta's meeting with a known Iraqi agent in Prague shortly before the attack and a facility in Iraq, equipped with a jetliner, that defectors report is used to train would-be hijackers.)

We have no choice but to . . . take . . . whatever steps are necessary to end Saddam's misrule and liberate the Iraqi people.

Saddam's large biological-weapons program is particularly ominous in light of the interest expressed by Atta and some of his colleagues in the use of crop dusters. . . . It is unclear whether there is more than coincidence in some of the apparent connections between those associated with the 9/11 attacks and the anthrax used against Florida-based tabloids, other media organizations and top congressional figures. (For example, one of the hijackers received medical treatment shortly before his death for what the attending physician believes may have been symptoms of cutaneous anthrax, and several of the hijackers rented an apartment from a woman married to an executive at one of the anthrax-targeted tabloids.)

It is safe to say, however, that had the particular strain of anthrax—of a sophisticated type that Iraq and very few other nations could produce—been delivered to Congress and the other recipients via crop duster instead of the U.S. Postal Service, there likely would have been many thousands of dead.

It would be in keeping with such efforts—in which cutouts appear to have been used by Saddam to inflict lethal blows on the United States while concealing Iraq's true role—if the "Butcher of Baghdad" were to try next to exploit America's complete vulnerability to missile attack. This could be done with catastrophic effect, thanks to the continuing absence of any deployed U.S. missile-defense system, should the Iraqi despot arrange to have one of the Scud missiles he is believed to have hidden from U.S. warplanes and U.N. inspectors launched from a third-country-registered ship operating off our coast.

The necessity of regime change

In short, today even more than in 1998, it is clear that the risk of Saddam engaging, either directly or indirectly, in the use of WMDs no longer safely can be ignored. Similarly, we now know that there is no practical alternative to regime change in Iraq if that threat is to be mitigated, let alone eliminated.

If anything, Saddam has been emboldened by successive U.S. administrations' failures to deal decisively with him and his reign of terror. He successfully has defied U.S. presidents, the United Nations, his treaty commitments and international law. He has worn down inspectors and sanction regimes, diplomats and no-fly zones. He has shown himself to be as resilient to unenforced claims that he is being kept in "his box" as he is to humanitarian appeals to use oil-for-food monies as they were intended—namely, to alleviate the suffering of the Iraqi people. He will make an even greater mockery of any so-called "smart-sanctions" regime, further corrupting and intimidating his neighbors as his wealth and power continue to be restored by Europeans, Russians and Chinese anxious to resume doing business with him.

For these reasons, we have no choice but to do what Rumsfeld, Wolfowitz and their colleagues recommended four years ago: Take at once whatever steps are necessary to end Saddam's misrule and liberate the Iraqi people. Unfortunately, we cannot be sure that such steps will result in the elimination of all Iraqi WMD programs. If we pursue the sort of strategy for accomplishing Saddam's downfall that was laid out by the Coalition for Peace and Security in the Gulf, however, it should end the threat they pose.

That means ruling out the notion of pursuing Saddam's downfall via a coup d'etat that very well could wind up merely replacing one dangerous Iraqi dictator with another, possibly equally odious, despot. The latter, however, could be freed from the constraints under which the Butcher of Baghdad currently operates simply because he is not Saddam. As the signatories of the coalition's open letter put it in 1998:

> For years, the United States has tried to remove Saddam by encouraging coups and internal conspiracies. These attempts have all failed. Saddam is more wily, brutal and conspiratorial than any likely conspiracy the United States might mobilize against him. Saddam must be overpowered; he will not be brought down by a coup d'etat. But Saddam has an Achilles' heel: lacking popular support, he rules by terror. The same brutality which makes it unlikely that any coups or conspiracies can succeed makes him hated by his own people and the rank and file of his military. Iraq today is ripe for a broad-based insurrection. We must exploit this opportunity.

Political and military strategies

Instead, the Committee for Peace and Security in the Gulf recommended "a comprehensive political and military strategy for bringing down Saddam and his regime." Specifically, it proposed that the United States: a) "recognize a provisional government of Iraq based on the principles and leaders of the Iraqi National Congress that is representative of all the peoples of Iraq"; b) "restore and enhance the safe haven in northern Iraq to allow the provisional government to extend its authority there and establish a zone in southern Iraq from which Saddam's ground forces would also be excluded"; and c) "lift sanctions in liberated areas."

The last of these is particularly noteworthy. As the committee's signatories observed: "Sanctions are instruments of war against Saddam's regime, but they should be quickly lifted on those who have freed themselves from it." Also, the oil resources and products of the liberated areas should help fund the provisional government's insurrection and humanitarian relief for the people of liberated Iraq, as should unfrozen "Iraqi assets—which amount to $1.6 billion in the United States and Britain alone" that can help "the provisional government to fund its insurrection."

Importantly, the committee acknowledged that the United States had a responsibility to "help expand liberated areas of Iraq by assisting the provisional government's offensive against Saddam Hussein's regime logistically and through other means." The signatories counseled that "a systematic air campaign [be launched] against the pillars of [Saddam's] power—the Republican Guard divisions which prop him up and the military infrastructure that sustains him." They also recommended that "U.S. ground-force equipment [be positioned] in the region so that, as a last resort, we have the capacity to protect and assist the anti-Saddam forces in the northern and southern parts of Iraq."

This prescription for effecting regime change in Iraq would have the advantage of empowering the Iraqi people to help liberate themselves with a minimum of U.S. military involvement and risk. It is past time it be given a chance to work. Indeed, we no longer can afford to do otherwise.

8

A U.S. Invasion of Iraq Is Not Justified

Stephen Zunes

Stephen Zunes is an associate professor of politics at the University of San Francisco, Middle East editor of the Foreign Policy in Focus website (www.fpif.org), and the author of Tinder Box: U.S. Middle East Policy and the Roots of Terrorism.

A U.S. invasion of Iraq is not justified because there is no credible evidence that the Iraqi government supports terrorism, has developed an arsenal of weapons of mass destruction, or intends to harm U.S. interests through military action. Moreover, a U.S. invasion of Iraq would be based on President George W. Bush's declaration that the United States has the right to invade any country hostile to its interests. Such a stance would undermine the system of international law and order developed since World War I. Only the United Nations can sanction military action against Iraq, and there are insufficient grounds for it to do so. Invading Iraq would also incite further anti-American sentiments in the Middle East and would increase threats to America's security.

Despite growing opposition, both at home and abroad, the George W. Bush Administration appears to have begun its concerted final push to convince Congress, the American people and the world of the need to invade Iraq. Such an invasion would constitute an important precedent, being the first test of the new doctrine articulated by President Bush of "pre-emption," which declares that the United States has the right to invade sovereign countries and overthrow their governments if they are seen as hostile to American interests. At stake is not just the prospect of a devastating war but the very legitimacy of an international system built over the past century that—despite its failings—has created at least some semblance of global order and stability.

It is therefore critical to examine and rebut the Administration's arguments, because if as fundamental a policy decision as whether to go to war cannot be influenced by the active input of an informed citizenry, what also may be at stake is nothing less than American democracy, at least in any meaningful sense of the word.

Below are the eight principal arguments put forward by proponents of a US invasion of Iraq, each followed by a rebuttal.

Iraq and terrorism

1. Iraq is providing support for Al Qaeda [the terrorist group held responsible for the September 11, 2001, terrorist attacks] and is a center for anti-American terrorism.

The Bush Administration has failed to produce credible evidence that the Iraqi regime has any links whatsoever with Al Qaeda. None of the September 11 hijackers were Iraqi, no major figure in Al Qaeda is Iraqi, nor has any part of Al Qaeda's money trail been traced to Iraq. Investigations by the FBI, the CIA and Czech intelligence have found no substance to rumors of a meeting in spring 2001 between one of the September 11 hijackers and an Iraqi intelligence operative in Prague. It is highly unlikely that the decidedly secular Baathist regime—which has savagely suppressed Islamists within Iraq—would be able to maintain close links with [al Qaeda terrorist] Osama bin Laden and his followers. Saudi Prince Turki bin Faisal, his country's former intelligence chief, has noted that bin Laden views Saddam Hussein "as an apostate, an infidel, or someone who is not worthy of being a fellow Muslim." In fact, bin Laden offered in 1990 to raise an army of thousands of mujahedeen fighters to liberate Kuwait from Iraqi occupation.

The State Department's . . . annual study, Patterns of Global Terrorism, *could not list any serious act of international terrorism connected to the government of Iraq.*

There have been credible reports of extremist Islamist groups operating in northern Iraq, but these are exclusively within Kurdish areas, which have been outside Baghdad's control since the end of the Gulf War. Iraq's past terrorist links are limited to such secular groups as the one led by Abu Nidal, a now largely defunct Palestinian faction opposed to Yasir Arafat's Palestine Liberation Organization. Ironically, at the height of Iraq's support of Abu Nidal in the early 1980s, Washington dropped Iraq from its list of terrorism-sponsoring countries so the United States could bolster Iraq's war effort against Iran. Baghdad was reinstated to the list only after the Iraqi invasion of Kuwait in 1990, even though US officials were unable to cite increased Iraqi ties to terrorism.

The State Department's own annual study, *Patterns of Global Terrorism,* could not list any serious act of international terrorism connected to the government of Iraq. A recent CIA report indicates that the Iraqis have been consciously avoiding any actions against the United States or its facilities abroad, presumably to deny Washington any excuse to engage in further military strikes against their country. The last clear example that American officials can cite of Iraqi-backed terrorism was an alleged plot by Iraqi agents to assassinate former President George Bush when he visited Kuwait in 1993. (In response, President Bill Clinton ordered the bombing of Baghdad, hitting an Iraqi intelligence headquarters as well as a nearby civilian neighborhood.)

An American invasion of Iraq would not only distract from the more immediate threat posed by Al Qaeda but would likely result in an anti-American backlash that would substantially reduce the level of cooperation from Islamic countries in tracking down and neutralizing the remaining Al Qaeda cells. Indeed, the struggle against terrorism is too important to be sabotaged by ideologues obsessed with settling old scores.

The Iraqi threat has been exaggerated

2. Containment has failed.

While some countries, in part due to humanitarian concerns, are circumventing economic sanctions against Iraq, the military embargo appears to be holding solid. It was only as a result of the import of technology and raw materials from Russia, Germany, France, Britain and the United States that Iraq was able to develop its biological, chemical and nuclear weapons programs in the 1980s.

Iraq's armed forces are barely one-third their pre–Gulf War strength. Even though Iraq has not been required to reduce its conventional forces, the destruction of its weapons and the country's economic collapse have led to a substantial reduction in men under arms. Iraq's navy is now virtually nonexistent, and its air force is just a fraction of what it was before the war. Military spending by Iraq has been estimated at barely one-tenth of what it was in the 1980s. The Bush Administration has been unable to explain why today, when Saddam has only a tiny percentage of his once-formidable military capability, Iraq is now considered such a threat that it is necessary to invade the country and replace its leader—the same leader Washington quietly supported during the peak of Iraq's military capability.

The International Atomic Energy Agency declared in 1998 that Iraq's nuclear program had been completely dismantled. The UN Special Commission on Iraq (UNSCOM) estimated then that at least 95 percent of Iraq's chemical weapons program had been similarly accounted for and destroyed. Iraq's potential to develop biological weapons is a much bigger question mark, since such a program is much easier to hide. However, UNSCOM noted in 1998 that virtually all of Iraq's offensive missiles and other delivery systems had been accounted for and rendered inoperable. Rebuilding an offensive military capability utilizing weapons of mass destruction (WMDs) virtually from scratch would be extraordinarily difficult under the current international embargo.

3. Deterrence will not work against a Saddam Hussein with weapons of mass destruction.

Saddam Hussein has demonstrated repeatedly that he cares first and foremost about his own survival. He presumably recognizes that any attempt to use WMDs against the United States or any of its allies would inevitably lead to his own destruction. This is why he did not use them during the Gulf War, even when attacked by the largest coalition of international forces against a single nation ever assembled and subjected to the heaviest bombing in world history. By contrast, prior to the Gulf

War, Saddam was quite willing to utilize his arsenal of chemical weapons against Iranian forces because he knew the revolutionary Islamist regime was isolated internationally, and he was similarly willing to use them against Kurdish civilians because he knew they could not fight back. In the event of a US invasion, however, seeing his overthrow as imminent and with nothing to lose, this logic of self-preservation would no longer be operative. Instead, a US invasion—rather than eliminate the prospect of Iraq using its WMDs—would in fact dramatically increase the likelihood of his utilizing weapons of mass destruction should he actually have any at his disposal.

Saddam Hussein's leadership style has always been that of direct control; his distrust of subordinates (bordering on paranoia) is one of the ways he has been able to hold on to power. It is extremely unlikely that he would go to the risk and expense of developing weapons of mass destruction only to pass them on to some group of terrorists, particularly radical Islamists who could easily turn on him. If he does have such weapons at his disposal, they would be for use at his discretion alone. By contrast, in the chaos of a US invasion and its aftermath, the chances of such weapons being smuggled out of the country into the hands of terrorists would greatly increase. Currently, any Iraqi WMDs that may exist are under the control of a highly centralized regime more interested in deterring a US attack than provoking one.

A US invasion . . . would in fact dramatically increase the likelihood of [Saddam Hussein's] utilizing weapons of mass destruction.

---

4. International inspectors cannot insure that Iraq will not obtain weapons of mass destruction.

As a result of the inspections regime imposed by the United Nations at the end of the Gulf War, virtually all of Iraq's stockpile of WMDs, delivery systems and capability of producing such weapons were destroyed. During nearly eight years of operation, UNSCOM oversaw the destruction of 38,000 chemical weapons, 480,000 liters of live chemical-weapons agents, forty-eight missiles, six missile launchers, thirty missile warheads modified to carry chemical or biological agents, and hundreds of pieces of related equipment with the capability to produce chemical weapons.

In late 1997 UNSCOM director Richard Butler reported that UNSCOM had made "significant progress" in tracking Iraq's chemical weapons program and that 817 of the 819 Soviet-supplied long-range missiles had been accounted for. A couple of dozen Iraqi-made ballistic missiles remained unaccounted for, but these were of questionable caliber. In its last three years of operation, UNSCOM was unable to detect any evidence that Iraq had been concealing prohibited weapons.

The periodic interference and harassment of UNSCOM inspectors by the Iraqis was largely limited to sensitive sites too small for advanced nuclear or chemical weapons development or deployment. A major reason for this lack of cooperation was Iraqi concern—later proven valid—that the United States was abusing the inspections for espionage purposes, such as monitoring coded radio communications by Iraq's security forces, using equipment secretly installed by American inspectors. The United States, eager to launch military strikes against Iraq, instructed Butler in 1998 to provoke Iraq into breaking its agreement to fully cooperate with UNSCOM. Without consulting the UN Security Council as required, Butler announced to the Iraqis that he was nullifying agreements dealing with sensitive sites and chose the Baath Party headquarters in Baghdad—a very unlikely place to store weapons of mass destruction—as the site at which to demand unfettered access. The Iraqis refused. Clinton then asked Butler to withdraw UNSCOM forces, and the United States launched a four-day bombing campaign, which gave the Iraqis an excuse to block UNSCOM inspectors from returning. With no international inspectors in Iraq since then, there is no definitive answer as to whether Iraq is actually developing weapons of mass destruction. And as long as the United States continues to openly espouse "regime change" through assassination or invasion, it is very unlikely that Iraq will agree to a resumption of inspections.

International law

5. The United States has the legal right to impose a regime change through military force.

According to Articles 41 and 42 of the UN Charter, no member state has the right to enforce any resolution militarily unless the Security Council determines that there has been a material breach of its resolution, decides that all nonmilitary means of enforcement have been exhausted and specifically authorizes the use of military force. This is what the Security Council did in November 1990 with Resolution 678 in response to Iraq's occupation of Kuwait, which violated a series of resolutions demanding their withdrawal that passed that August. When Iraq finally complied in its forced withdrawal from Kuwait in March 1991, this resolution became moot.

Legally, the conflict regarding access for UN inspectors and possible Iraqi procurement of WMDs has always been between the Iraqi government and the UN, not between Iraq and the United States. Although UN Security Council Resolution 687, which demands Iraqi disarmament, was the most detailed in the world body's history, no military enforcement mechanisms were specified. Nor has the Security Council specified any military enforcement mechanisms in subsequent resolutions. As is normally the case when it is determined that governments are violating all or part of UN resolutions, any decision about enforcement is a matter for the Security Council as a whole—not for any one member of the Council.

If the United States can unilaterally claim the right to invade Iraq because of that country's violation of Security Council resolutions, other Council members could logically also claim the right to invade states that are similarly in violation; for example, Russia could claim the right to invade Israel, France could claim the right to invade Turkey and Britain could claim the right to invade Morocco. The US insistence on the right to attack unilaterally could seriously undermine the principle of collective security and the authority of the UN and, in doing so, would open the door to international anarchy.

International law is quite clear about when military force is allowed. In addition to the aforementioned case of UN Security Council authorization, the only other time that a member state is allowed to use armed force is described in Article 51, which states that it is permissible for "individual or collective self-defense" against "armed attack . . . until the Security Council has taken measures necessary to maintain international peace and security." If Iraq's neighbors were attacked, any of these countries could call on the United States to help, pending a Security Council decision authorizing the use of force.

There [are not] sufficient legal grounds for the United States to convince the [UN] Security Council to approve the use of military force against Iraq.

Based on evidence that the Bush Administration has made public, there doesn't appear to be anything close to sufficient legal grounds for the United States to convince the Security Council to approve the use of military force against Iraq in US self-defense.

The costs of invading

6. The benefits of regime change outweigh the costs.

While the United States would likely be the eventual victor in a war against Iraq, it would come at an enormous cost. It would be a mistake, for example, to think that defeating Iraq would result in as few American casualties as occurred in driving the Taliban militia from Kabul. Though Iraq's offensive capabilities have been severely weakened by the bombings, sanctions and UNSCOM-sponsored decommissioning, its defensive military capabilities are still strong.

Nor would a military victory today be as easy as during the Gulf War. Prior to the launching of Operation Desert Storm, the Iraqi government decided not to put up a fight for Kuwait and relied mostly on young conscripts from minority communities. Only two of the eight divisions of the elite Republican Guard were ever in Kuwait, and they pulled back before the war began. The vast majority of Iraq's strongest forces were withdrawn to areas around Baghdad to fight for the survival of the regime itself, and they remain there to this day. In the event of war, defections from these units are not likely.

Close to 1 million members of the Iraqi elite have a vested interest in the regime's survival. These include the Baath Party leadership and its supporters, security and intelligence personnel, and core elements of the armed forces and their extended families. Furthermore, Iraq—a largely urban society—has a far more sophisticated infrastructure than does the largely rural and tribal Afghanistan, and it could be mobilized in the event of a foreign invasion.

Nor is there an equivalent to Afghanistan's Northern Alliance, which did the bulk of the ground fighting against the Taliban. Iraqi Kurds, having been abandoned twice in recent history by the United States, are unlikely to fight beyond securing autonomy for Kurdish areas. The armed

Shiite opposition has largely been eliminated, and it too would be unlikely to fight beyond liberating the majority Shiite sections of southern Iraq. The United States would be reluctant to support either, given that their successes could potentially fragment the country and would encourage both rebellious Kurds in southeastern Turkey and restive Shiites in northeastern Saudi Arabia. US forces would have to march on Baghdad, a city of more than 5 million people, virtually alone.

Unlike in the Gulf War, which involved conventional and open combat in flat desert areas where US and allied forces could take full advantage of their superior firepower and technology, US soldiers would have to fight their way through heavily populated agricultural and urban lands. Invading forces would likely be faced with bitter, house-to-house fighting in a country larger than South Vietnam. Iraqis, who may have had little stomach to fight to maintain their country's conquest of Kuwait, would be far more willing to sacrifice themselves to resist a foreign, Western invader. To minimize American casualties in the face of such stiff resistance, the United States would likely engage in heavy bombing of Iraqi residential neighborhoods, resulting in high civilian casualties.

The lack of support from regional allies could result in the absence of a land base from which to launch US air attacks, initially requiring the United States to rely on Navy jets launched from aircraft carriers. Without permission to launch aerial refueling craft, even long-range bombers from US air bases might not be deployable. It is hard to imagine being able to provide the necessary reconnaissance and surveillance aircraft under such circumstances, and the deployment of tens of thousands of troops from distant staging areas could be problematic. American forces could conceivably capture an air base inside Iraq in the course of the fighting, but without the pre-positioning of supplies, its usefulness as a major center of operations would be marginal.

The United States would likely engage in heavy bombing of Iraqi residential neighborhoods, resulting in high civilian casualties.

Such a major military operation would be costly in economic terms as well, as the struggling and debt-ridden US economy would be burdened by the most elaborate and expensive deployment of American forces since World War II, totaling more than $100 billion in the first six months. Unlike in the Gulf War, the Saudis—who strenuously oppose such an invasion—would be unwilling to foot the bill. An invasion of Iraq would also be costly to a struggling world economy; higher oil prices could be devastating to some countries, causing even more social and political unrest.

Fueling anti-American sentiments in the Middle East

7. Regime change will be popular in Iraq and will find support among US allies in the region.

While there is little question that most of Iraq's neighbors and most Iraqis themselves would be pleased to see Iraq under new leadership, regime change imposed by invading US military forces would not be welcome. Most US allies in the region supported the Gulf War, since it was widely viewed as an act of collective security in response to aggression by Iraq against its small neighbor. This would not be the case, however, in the event of a new war against Iraq. Saudi Crown Prince Abdullah has warned that the Bush Administration "should not strike Iraq, because such an attack would only raise animosity in the region against the United States." At the Beirut summit of the Arab League, the Arab nations unanimously endorsed a strongly worded resolution opposing an attack against Iraq. Even Kuwait has reconciled with Iraq since Baghdad formally recognized Kuwait's sovereignty and international borders. Twenty Arab foreign ministers meeting in Cairo unanimously expressed their "total rejection of the threat of aggression on Arab nations, in particular Iraq."

American officials claim that, public statements to the contrary, there may be some regional allies willing to support a US war effort. Given President Bush's ultimatum that "either you are with us or you are with the terrorists," it's quite possible that some governments will be successfully pressured to go along. However, almost any Middle Eastern regime willing to provide such support and cooperation would be doing so over the opposition of the vast majority of its citizens. Given the real political risks for any ruler supporting the US war effort, such acquiescence would take place only reluctantly, as a result of US pressure or inducements, not from a sincere belief in the validity of the military operation.

8. "Regime change" will enhance regional stability and enhance the prospects for democracy in the region.

As is apparent in Afghanistan, throwing a government out is easier than putting a new one together. Although most Iraqis would presumably be relieved in the event of Saddam Hussein's ouster, this does not mean that a regime installed by a Western army would be welcomed. For example, some of the leading candidates that US officials are apparently considering installing to govern Iraq following a successful US invasion are former Iraqi military officers who took part in offensives that involved war crimes.

In addition to possible ongoing guerrilla action by Saddam Hussein's supporters, American occupation forces would likely be faced with competing armed factions among the Sunni Arab population, not to mention Kurdish and Shiite rebel groups seeking greater autonomy. This could lead the United States into a bloody counterinsurgency war. Without the support of other countries or the UN, a US invasion could leave American forces effectively alone attempting to enforce a peace amid the chaos of a post-Saddam Iraq.

A US invasion of Iraq would likely lead to an outbreak of widespread anti-American protests throughout the Middle East, perhaps even attacks against American interests. Some pro-Western regimes could become vulnerable to internal radical forces. Passions are particularly high in light of strong US support for the policies of Israel's rightist government and its ongoing occupation of the West Bank and Gaza Strip. The anger over US double standards regarding Israeli and Iraqi violations of UN Security Council resolutions and possession of weapons of mass destruction could reach a boiling point. Recognizing that the United States cannot be defeated on the battlefield, more and more Arabs and Muslims resentful of American hegemony in their heartland may be prone to attack by unconventional means, as was so tragically demonstrated September 11, 2001. The Arab foreign ministers, aware of such possibilities, warned at their meeting in Cairo that a US invasion of Iraq would "open the gates of hell."

9

The United States Should Assassinate Some Leaders of Rogue States and Terrorist Groups

Richard Lowry

Richard Lowry is editor of the National Review, *a conservative weekly magazine.*

U.S. leaders are uncomfortable discussing it, but assassination is a morally justifiable means of dealing with enemy heads of state during wartime. Under international law, the targeted killing of specific individuals is legal during wartime, and in moral terms, killing a single leader through assassination is preferable to killing thousands of soldiers on the battlefield. America's hesitancy to openly condone assassination is due to executive order 12333, issued by former President Gerald Ford, which prohibits assassination by agents of the U.S. government. In the war on terrorism, however, assassination is an effective and justifiable means of dealing with foreign leaders who support terrorism.

After Iraqi leader Saddam Hussein invaded Kuwait in 1990, President George H.W. Bush signed a secret finding authorizing the CIA to attempt to overthrow the Iraqi dictator. Bob Woodward reports in his book *The Commanders* that "the CIA was not to violate the ban on involvement in assassination attempts, but rather recruit Iraqi dissidents to remove Saddam from power." In other words, according to the strict letter of the finding, Saddam was to be ousted not "dead or alive," but only alive—at least as far as the CIA had any control over it.

Around the same time, defense secretary Dick Cheney fired Air Force chief of staff Michael J. Dugan for telling reporters that the U.S. wanted to "decapitate" the Iraqi regime by killing Saddam and his family. Dugan was sacked not just for revealing operational details, Cheney explained, but also for speaking favorably about a policy that might violate the ban on assassinations. "We never talk about the targeting of specific individuals who are officials of other governments," Cheney said.

Why this tender concern for Saddam Hussein's well-being? It was part of a hangover from the implosion of America's moral self-confidence that occurred in the 1970s, in the wake of Vietnam and the Church committee's battering of the CIA as a hapless, dirty-tricks operation. The Gerald Ford administration, bowing to congressional pressure, rushed to issue an executive order banning assassination. During the Gulf War, the first Bush administration didn't let its regard for the Ford order actually stop it from bombing Saddam's personal compounds, but it pretended not to have entertained the idea of specifically killing him.

America's misguided ban on assassination

This garble reflects a lack of exactly the sort of clarity that the war on terrorism demands: Killing enemy belligerents, even if they are heads of state, is a lawful and moral application of American power. The Ford order on assassinations—reissued by Ronald Reagan as Executive Order 12333—should either be amended, or at the very least publicly reinterpreted, so there is no longer any confusion on this point. It is the right of the U.S. to target and kill individuals in the chain of command of a country with which we are formally, or as a practical matter, at war.

The upshot of the Church committee's work in 1975 was that after 30 years of the twilight struggle, the United States should get out of the twilight business. The Cold War consensus had been based on the idea that our enemy was evil and ruthless, and therefore we would have to employ rough means to defeat it (as a commission headed by Herbert Hoover put it starkly in 1954, "hitherto acceptable norms of human conduct do not apply").

The Church committee was devoted to the proposition that engaging in such nasty business made us no better—actually, somehow much worse—than the Soviets. "The committee was struck," said the Church report, "by the basic tension—if not incompatibility—of covert operations and the demands of the constitutional system." The U.S. should worry more about its virtue and less about power politics. "We need not be so frightened by each Russian intervention," Senator Frank Church said. "We have gained little, and lost a great deal, by our past policy of compulsive interventionism."

From this aloof perspective on world affairs, the committee concluded that "assassination is unacceptable in our society." Period. It dredged up stories of far-fetched attempts to off Fidel Castro—poisoned cigars, poisoned diving suits—that made assassination seem a risible exercise (as if the fact that we were bad at assassination proved that we should never do it). It also focused on shadowy U.S. involvement in the killings in the 1950s and 1960s of Patrice Lumumba in Congo, Rafael Trujillo in the Dominican Republic, and Ngo Dinh Diem in Vietnam.

The committee had a point. There were questions about whether the CIA was operating with the necessary democratic accountability in the U.S., and these killings took place over what essentially amounted to peacetime political preferences (although peacetime was difficult to define in the Cold War, since the Soviets envisioned it as just another opportunity to wage war). So, these acts were more properly thought of as unlawful assassinations rather than legitimate wartime killings.

In judging such killings, as former Reagan and Bush official David Rivkin points out, this is really the crucial distinction: between peace and war. From the Romans to the U.N. Charter, international law has recognized certain "protected persons"—heads of state, diplomats—who can't be killed by a foreign power in peacetime. But, as Rivkin says, "war changes everything." There is a right under international law to target an enemy's command and control during wartime, including anyone in the chain of command right up to the head of state (especially when, as in the case of Saddam, he wears a uniform and a sidearm).

Why, then, does such an odor still attach to targeting specific individuals in wartime? It is partly a leftover from 18th- and 19th-century rules of warfare, when battle was essentially an interruption of otherwise correct relations between fellow sovereigns. As Notre Dame law professor Gerard V. Bradley points out, it wouldn't have occurred to the French, for instance, to try to kill William Pitt. It just wasn't done. But this all changed with the advent of total war, and of leaders, such as Adolf Hitler, unfit for the chummy "community of nations."

In June 1943, the Germans shot down what they took to be British prime minister Winston Churchill's plane. Two months before, the Americans had shot down Admiral Isoroku Yamamoto's plane, after an intelligence intercept revealed that he would be inspecting front-line Japanese bases. Admiral Nimitz carefully considered whether any of Yamamoto's possible replacements would be worse—i.e., more talented or better liked by Japanese troops—and, after concluding they wouldn't, ordered the attack. No one at the time complained that this act was incompatible with American values.

Legality and morality

The hesitation to endorse such targeted killings today—when we are a century and several million deaths beyond the age of international chivalry—involves a misunderstanding of what exactly is proscribed by international law. According to Article 23b of the Hague Convention, "It is especially forbidden to kill or wound treacherously individuals belonging to the hostile nation or army." This is not, however, a prohibition on all targeted killings. Instead, for a killing to be considered an unlawful assassination, it has to use treacherous means.

Killing enemy belligerents, even if they are heads of state, is a lawful and moral application of American power.

Treachery is an extremely narrow concept. In current practice, we seem, oddly, to interpret it as anything that would be too precise or sneaky. So, killing Saddam Hussein with a barrage of guided bombs, as long as we are not too frank about whether his death is intended or not, is acceptable (not treacherous), but killing him with one cruise missile aimed right at his bedroom, or, even worse, shooting him with a sniper team or setting a booby trap in front of his motorcade, is forbidden (treacherous). This from-15,000-feet rule is as irrational as it sounds.

In fact, any method that is lawful for attacking an enemy army is also lawful as a way of killing an enemy leader. The use of perfidious means to take advantage of a target's trust—such as disguising a U.S. hit team as U.N. negotiators—is forbidden. (Terrorist Osama Bin Laden's use of assassins posing as journalists to kill Afghanistan's Northern Alliance leader Ahmed Massoud is a classic case of perfidy.) Otherwise, there is nothing that says targeted killings must take place from the air. As the U.S. Army Memorandum of Law puts it, "No distinction is made between an attack accomplished by aircraft, missile, naval gunfire, artillery, mortar, infantry assault, ambush . . . booby trap, a single shot by a sniper, a commando attack, or other similar means."

It's odd to consider it unacceptable to kill Saddam [Hussein], but acceptable to kill thousands of his soldiers.

International law aside, the morality of targeted wartime killings, when compared with other possible policies, seems obvious. Such killings are clearly superior to the Left's preferred non-violent means of trying to oust dictators: economic sanctions. Such embargoes almost always punish the innocent (civilians of the targeted country) and sometimes even strengthen the guilty (the dictators who are able to play the besieged victim). In Iraq, sanctions have—if anything—helped impoverish the civilian population, without budging Saddam a bit.

Targeted killing can also be morally superior to waging all-out war. One of the reasons the Geneva Convention protects POWs is that soldiers are held blameless for state policies that they were presumably merely following, not creating. So, it's odd to consider it unacceptable to kill Saddam, but acceptable to kill thousands of his soldiers who may want nothing more fervently than to surrender to the nearest American. Indeed, the idea of proportionality in the law of war suggests that the means able to achieve an objective with the least destruction and killing—e.g., specifically targeting Saddam—is always to be preferred.

Practical objections

Critics of targeted killings still raise several practical objections to the idea. One is that it would prompt retaliation against U.S. leaders. But Saddam Hussein has already tried to kill an ex-U.S. president, Bush I in Kuwait City, even with EO12333 still in force. And Osama bin Laden launched a hijacked airplane perhaps against the White House or the U.S. Capitol. The behavior of our enemies obviously isn't going to be positively influenced by our nice legalisms. In any case, the American president is now, and always will be, surrounded by the most sophisticated and tightest security in the world, executive order or no.

Another objection is that targeted killings simply don't make for good foreign policy. They fail and backfire. Even if they succeed, the resulting new regime can be hard to predict and control. All of this is true, and if we want to influence the course of a post-Saddam Iraq, an invasion six months from now may be preferable to killing Saddam tomorrow. But this doesn't mean that targeted killing shouldn't be an option. And, in the case of Iraq, an incipient invasion (giving us a military presence to control events on the ground) coupled with the killing of Saddam (to end the fighting quickly) may be the ideal scenario.

In the end, critics of the idea of targeted killings fall back on the assertion that it is somehow incompatible with American values. This is just Frank Churchism, a moral equivalence that condemns us for trying to kill first the people who are bent on killing us. It finds it intolerable that we might engage in any difficult or severe action in the course of defeating our mortal enemies, and perversely revels in any mistake, folly, or transgression we might commit along the way. It is this sensibility that splashes every American error in Afghanistan across the front pages, with the revelatory subtext that—aha!—we aren't so right and just after all.

[The September 11, 2001, terrorist attacks on America have] helped diminish, but not vanquish, this way of thinking. The Bill Clinton administration initially wanted to try Osama bin Laden, then attempted to kill him by arguing that he was, in effect, a piece of terrorist "infrastructure" to be "degraded." The George W. Bush administration has taken a leap ahead in clarity by frankly stating that Osama bin Laden is a person, just an evil one who deserves to be sent to his eternal reward as quickly as possible. As a terrorist bandit, bin Laden enjoys the protection of no international conventions against assassination or anything else. The same should go for Saddam Hussein, and other leaders in the future against whom we wage war.

For practical purposes, the ban on assassinations has recently eroded. The U.S. has over the last 15 years slyly targeted [Libyan strongman Muammar] Qaddafi, Saddam, [Serbian president Slobodan] Milosevic, and now Mullah Omar. But we should stop operating under the constraints of the Qaddafi rule, which holds essentially that if an attack on a leader is so imprecise that it might kill his friends and family, it's okay. The cleanest solution would be to add a definition of assassination to the executive order, making it clear that it doesn't forbid targeting a regime's military elite. This might offend the sensibilities of rogue-state leaders the world over, but so what?

"Rogue state" isn't just an idle phrase. It signifies a government that is operating outside of all civilized bounds. The U.S. now seems to be willing, not just to recognize this fact rhetorically, but to act on it with a policy of regime-change—which makes it very odd that we would insist on maintaining the polite norms of long ago, when every sovereign was a sort of brother. Saddam Hussein is a far cry from William Pitt. It is time we stop pretending otherwise.

10

The United States Should Not Assassinate Leaders of Rogue States and Terrorist Groups

Ward Thomas

Ward Thomas is an assistant professor of political science at the College of the Holy Cross and an associate of the John M. Olin Institute of Strategic Studies at Harvard University.

In the wake of the September 11, 2001, terrorist attacks on America, some pundits and legislators have proposed nullifying the executive order that forbids U.S. agents from taking part in assassinations. Doing so would hinder the war on terrorism more than it would help. Assassination is illegal under international law; therefore, adopting it would alienate potential allies. Moreover, to openly condone assassination would be to legitimate a practice that is currently the province of rogue states and the terrorists themselves. International law does permit states engaged in armed conflict to kill combatants—including enemy leaders—using traditional military tactics, and this is not viewed as assassination. The United States should take advantage of this latitude within international law rather than openly flaunting it.

In the first days of the 107th Congress, Representative Bob Barr, Republican of Georgia, introduced the ambitiously titled Terrorist Elimination Act of 2001 that would nullify the 25-year-old executive order that forbids US employees from plotting or taking part in assassination. The bill attracted no cosponsors, appeared on no committee agendas, and garnered no support from the incoming George W. Bush administration.

But after the [September 11, 2001, terrorist attacks on America], and the looming specter of terrorist Osama bin Laden, the assassination question no longer languishes in obscurity.

The reasoning reflected in the bill and in the rising debate is not new and in fact continues a decades-old trend. The norm against assassinating foreign enemies, once so widely and reflexively accepted that it shielded even Napoleon and Adolf Hitler, has come under pressure as changes in the international system make it seem increasingly anachronistic. One such development has been the emergence of challenges such as guerrilla warfare and terrorism, against which traditional military responses have often proved inadequate. Thus, contemporary observers are far more likely than those of centuries past to object to the disconnect between killing tens of thousands of conscripts in battle while recoiling from the idea of targeting one or a few culpable individuals. In light of recent events, this anomaly seems even more unbalanced.

Killing those responsible for the attacks may, moreover, be the only way of neutralizing the danger they pose. Terrorists are immune to most of the diplomatic and economic pressures that can be brought to bear on sovereign states, and they have no real domestic constituency to answer to. While bringing the responsible parties to trial may appeal to our sense of lawfulness, there are serious problems with relying exclusively on a judicial approach. It may well be impossible to indict and convict these individuals without compromising intelligence sources that would be indispensable to protecting against future attacks. Indeed, it's both unrealistic and undesirable to expect that intelligence efforts proceed with an eye toward whether information would be admissible in a court of law.

Most fundamentally, even a spate of convictions would not cripple the organizations that pose the threat—a threat that, while it eludes easy categorization, is better understood in military than in criminal justice terms. If terrorist leaders are captured, of course, they must be tried, but the trials should be in addition to, not in lieu of, the destruction of the networks they command.

Reasons to keep the assassination ban

All this might seem to recommend assassination as serving principles of sound strategy, as well as those of retributive justice and economy of force. Still, there are good reasons for the United States to hesitate before rushing to adopt assassination as a foreign policy tool—reasons that have little to do with the morality of the practice. First, doing so would divert institutional focus within American intelligence agencies away from intelligence collection and analysis and toward covert operations. This would have been a problem even before Sept. 11, but now the stakes are inestimably higher, as Americans' faith in the intelligence community's ability to perform its core mission has been understandably shaken.

Lifting the assassination ban might remove a constraint, but it would also likely create distracting controversies over the proper balance between covert activities and the more mundane but essential task of intelligence gathering. Such disputes plagued the CIA during its Cold War–era flirtation with assassination. Now is not the time to give intelligence agencies uncertain marching orders.

Second, assassination runs counter to both international law and the norms of the international community. (The executive order is legally redundant; international customary and treaty law already outlaw assassination.) While it seems naive to worry about such matters at a time of crisis like this, failure to do so would likely prove shortsighted. Uprooting terrorist networks cannot be accomplished solely by military means, nor can that be accomplished quickly. This means that the success of US policy will continue to hinge heavily on winning and maintaining the backing of other nations, most critically Islamic states.

Third, and perhaps most important, the United States and its allies have a significant long-term stake in the stigma against assassination. In effect, the norm helps limit what is considered the legitimate practice of international violence to the methods at which these states excel: conventional military operations. By contrast, assassination is a classic "weapon of the weak": a low-tech, small-scale technique that places a premium on opaque secrecy and fanatical resolve.

Assassination is a classic "weapon of the weak": a low-tech, small-scale technique that places a premium on opaque secrecy and fanatical resolve.

Moreover, as an open society, the United States would probably be more vulnerable to assassination—and if history is a guide, less good at it—than those against whom it might be used. While some foes, including those the United States now confronts, will ignore norms anyway, it's prudent to think beyond current circumstances in deciding long-range policy. For this country to turn its back on the norm against assassination to eliminate a Saddam Hussein [Iraqi leader] would amount to reshuffling a deck that was stacked in its favor. How, then, does the nation go after terrorists without doing irreparable harm to other interests? A first step should be to better define the terms of the debate over assassination.

Use military force within the bounds of international law

What is often misunderstood is that the country need not reverse its current policy in order to use lethal force against terrorists. International law permits a state engaged in armed conflict to kill any legitimate combatant as long as the means used to do so are lawful—a proviso that would forbid, for example, gaining access to an enemy leader by false pretenses or attacking him with illegal weapons, but not targeting him with cruise missiles or uniformed snipers. Such actions might be seen as provocative, but no international lawyer would call it assassination.

The best option for the United States under the present circumstances is to obey international law scrupulously while taking advantage of the latitude it allows. This means shelving blustery talk about lifting the assassination ban, while at the same time aggressively targeting those responsible for the recent attacks within the context of military operations that adhere to the laws of war.

Doing things by the book is preferable for two reasons:

First, a lawful military response (along with diplomatic efforts) is better suited to the nature of the challenge, which is the existence of large and sophisticated terrorist networks rather than a handful of evil men.

Under the circumstances, simply taking out a few individuals at the top will not help much, and may make matters worse. Second, although some erosion of the norm against assassination may be inevitable, it would be far less pronounced than if the US government were to make a show of declaring that it will not be bound by international law.

While most countries support the United States in its determination to respond forcefully to the atrocities of Sept. 11, it is inevitable that freedom of action in the fight against terrorism will come at a cost, both diplomatic and moral. It would be folly to embrace a policy in the passions of the moment that both failed to address the fundamental problem and squandered the support of crucial elements of the international community. The United States cannot have the best of both worlds, but it must guard against ending up with the worst of both worlds.

11

The United States Should Use Military Force to Help Foster Democracy in the Middle East

Max Boot

Max Boot is the editorial features editor of the Wall Street Journal *and the author of* The Savage Wars of Peace: Small Wars and the Rise of American Power.

Many international observers have claimed that U.S. imperialism is partly to blame for global terrorism; for example, by providing assistance in the 1980s to Islamic fundamentalists in Afghanistan who opposed communism, the United States may have inadvertently strengthened the Taliban government that later harbored the al Qaeda terrorist network deemed responsible for the September 11, 2001, terrorist attacks. But in the war on terrorism, the United States should play a bigger, rather than a smaller, role in the internal affairs of Afghanistan and other "rogue" nations. Just as the British did in the nineteenth century, the United States, leading an international military force, could impose democratic state administrations in countries like Afghanistan and Iraq. This policy change would benefit not only the oppressed people living under despotic regimes, but would also constitute a major victory in the war on terror.

Many have suggested that the September 11, 2001, attack on America was payback for U.S. imperialism. If only we had not gone around sticking our noses where they did not belong, perhaps we would not now be contemplating a crater in lower Manhattan. The solution is obvious: The United States must become a kinder, gentler nation, must eschew quixotic missions abroad, must become, in Pat Buchanan's phrase, "a republic, not an empire." In fact this analysis is exactly backward: The September 11 attack was a result of *insufficient* American involvement and ambition; the solution is to be more expansive in our goals and more assertive in their implementation. It has been said, with the benefit of faulty hindsight, that America erred in providing the mujahedeen [Islamic holy warriors] with weapons and training that some of them now turn against us. But this was amply justified by the exigencies of the Cold War. The real problem is that we pulled out of Afghanistan after 1989. In so doing, the George H.W. Bush administration was following a classic realpolitik policy. We had gotten involved in this distant nation to wage a proxy war against the Soviet Union. Once that larger war was over, we could safely pull out and let the Afghans resolve their own affairs. And if the consequence was the rise of the Taliban—homicidal mullahs driven by a hatred of modernity itself—so what? Who cares who rules this flyspeck in Central Asia? So said the wise elder statesmen. The "so what" question has now been answered definitively; the answer lies in the rubble of the World Trade Center and Pentagon.

U.S. imperialism

We had better sense when it came to the Balkans, which could without much difficulty have turned into another Afghanistan. When Muslim Bosnians rose up against Serb oppression in the early 1990s, they received support from many of the same Islamic extremists who also backed the mujahedeen in Afghanistan. The Muslims of Bosnia are not particularly fundamentalist—after years of Communist rule, most are not all that religious—but they might have been seduced by the siren song of the mullahs if no one else had come to champion their cause. Luckily, someone else did. NATO and the United States intervened to stop the fighting in Bosnia, and later in Kosovo. Employing its leverage, the U.S. government pressured the Bosnian government into expelling the mujahedeen. [In early October 2001], NATO and Bosnian police arrested four men in Sarajevo suspected of links to international terrorist groups. Some Albanian hotheads next tried to stir up trouble in Macedonia, but, following the dispatch of a NATO peacekeeping force, they have now been pressured to lay down their arms. U.S. imperialism—a liberal and humanitarian imperialism, to be sure, but imperialism all the same—appears to have paid off in the Balkans.

Afghanistan and other troubled lands today cry out for the sort of enlightened foreign administration once provided by self-confident Englishmen.

The problem is that, while the Bill Clinton administration eventually did something right in the Balkans, elsewhere it was scandalously irresolute in the assertion of U.S. power. By cutting and running from Somalia after the deaths of 18 U.S. soldiers, Bill Clinton fostered a widespread impression that we could be chased out of a country by anyone who managed to kill a few Americans. (Ronald Reagan did much the same thing by pulling out of Lebanon after the 1983 bombing of the U.S. Marine barracks.) After the attacks on the U.S. embassies in Kenya and Tanzania in

1998, Clinton sent cruise missiles—not soldiers—to strike a symbolic blow against [terrorist Osama] bin Laden's training camps in Afghanistan and a pharmaceutical factory in Sudan. Those attacks were indeed symbolic, though not in the way Clinton intended. They symbolized not U.S. determination but rather passivity in the face of terrorism. And this impression was reinforced by the failure of either Bill Clinton or George W. Bush to retaliate for the attack on the *USS Cole* in October 2000, most likely carried out by Osama bin Laden's al Qaeda network. All these displays of weakness emboldened our enemies to commit greater and more outrageous acts of aggression, much as the failure of the West to contest Japan's occupation of Manchuria in the 1930s, or Mussolini's incursion into Abyssinia, encouraged the Axis powers toward more spectacular depravities.

The problem, in short, has not been excessive American assertiveness but rather insufficient assertiveness. The question is whether, having now been attacked, we will act as a great power should.

The legacy of British imperialism

It is striking—and no coincidence—that America now faces the prospect of military action in many of the same lands where generations of British colonial soldiers went on campaigns. Afghanistan, Sudan, Libya, Egypt, Arabia, Mesopotamia (Iraq), Palestine, Persia, the Northwest Frontier (Pakistan)—these are all places where, by the 19th century, ancient imperial authority, whether Ottoman, Mughal, or Safavid, was crumbling, and Western armies had to quell the resulting disorder. In Egypt, in 1882, Lieutenant General Sir Garnet Wolseley put down a nationalist revolt led by a forerunner of Nasser, Colonel Ahmed Arabi. In Sudan, in the 1880s, an early-day bin Laden who called himself the Mahdi (Messiah) rallied the Dervishes for a *jihad* to spread fundamentalist Islam to neighboring states. Mahdism was crushed by Sir Horatio Herbert Kitchener on the battlefield of Omdurman in 1889. Both Sudan and Egypt remained relatively quiet thereafter, until Britain finally pulled out after World War II.

In Afghanistan, the British suffered a serious setback in 1842 when their forces had to retreat from Kabul and were massacred—all but Dr. William Brydon, who staggered into Jalalabad to tell the terrible tale. This British failure has been much mentioned [in the weeks after September 11] to support the proposition that the Afghans are invincible fighters. Less remembered is the sequel. An army under Major General George Pollock forced the Khyber Pass, recaptured Kabul, burned down the Great Bazaar to leave "some lasting mark of the just retribution of an outraged nation," and then marched back to India.

Thirty-six years later, in 1878, the British returned to Afghanistan. The highlight of the Second Afghan War was Lieutenant General Frederick Roberts's once-famous march from Kabul to Kandahar. Although the British were always badly outnumbered, they repeatedly bested larger Afghan armies. The British did not try to impose a colonial administration in Kabul, but Afghanistan became in effect a British protectorate with its foreign policy controlled by the raj. This arrangement lasted until the Third Afghan War in 1919, when Britain, bled dry by World War I, finally left the Afghans to their own devices.

Afghanistan and other troubled lands today cry out for the sort of enlightened foreign administration once provided by self-confident Eng-lishmen in jodhpurs and pith helmets. Is imperialism a dusty relic of a long-gone era? Perhaps. But it's interesting to note that in the 1990s East Timor, Cambodia, Kosovo, and Bosnia all became wards of the interna-tional community (Cambodia only temporarily). This precedent could easily be extended, as suggested by David Rieff, into a formal system of United Nations mandates modeled on the mandatory territories sanc-tioned by the League of Nations in the 1920s. Following the defeat of the German and Ottoman empires, their colonial possessions were handed out to the Allied powers, in theory to prepare their inhabitants for even-tual self-rule. (America was offered its own mandate over Armenia, the Dardanelles, and Constantinople, but the Senate rejected it along with the Treaty of Versailles.) This was supposed to be "for the good of the na-tives," a phrase that once made progressives snort in derision, but may be taken more seriously after the left's conversion (or, rather, reversion) in the 1990s to the cause of "humanitarian" interventions.

State-building in Afghanistan

The mealy-mouthed modern euphemism is "nation-building," but "state building" is a better description. Building a national consciousness, while hardly impossible (the British turned a collection of princely states into modern India), is a long-term task. Building a working state administration is a more practical short-term objective that has been achieved by countless colonial regimes, including the United States in Haiti (1915–1933), the Do-minican Republic (1916–1924), Cuba (1899–1902, 1906–1909), and the Philippines (1899–1935), to say nothing of the achievements of generals Lucius Clay in Germany and Douglas MacArthur in Japan.

Unilateral U.S. rule may no longer be an option today. But the United States can certainly lead an international occupation force under U.N. auspices, with the cooperation of some Muslim nations. This would be a huge improvement in any number of lands that support or shelter ter-rorists. For the sake of simplicity, let's consider two: Afghanistan and Iraq.

We would not aim to impose our rule permanently. . . . Occupation would be a temporary expedient . . . until a responsible, humane, preferably democratic, government takes over.

In Afghanistan, . . . the Special Forces are said to be hunting [terror-ist] Osama bin Laden and his followers. Let us hope they do not catch him, at least not alive. It would not be an edifying spectacle to see this scourge of the infidels—this holy warrior who rejects the Enlightenment and all its works—asserting a medley of constitutional rights in a U.S. courtroom, perhaps even in the federal courthouse located just a short walk from where the World Trade Center once stood. But whatever hap-pens with bin Laden, it is clear we cannot leave the Taliban [who al-legedly sheltered bin Laden] in power. It is a regime that can bring noth-ing but grief to its people, its neighbors, and the United States.

But when we oust the Taliban, what comes next? Will we repeat our mistake of a decade ago and leave? What if no responsible government immediately emerges? What if millions of Afghans are left starving? Someone would have to step in and help—and don't bet on the U.N. High Commissioner for Refugees getting the job done. The United States, in cooperation with its allies, would be left with the responsibility to feed the hungry, tend the sick, and impose the rule of law. This is what we did for the defeated peoples of Germany, Italy, and Japan, and it is a service that we should extend to the oppressed people of Afghanistan as well. Unlike 19th-century European colonialists, we would not aim to impose our rule permanently. Instead, as in Western Germany, Italy, and Japan, occupation would be a temporary expedient to allow the people to get back on their feet until a responsible, humane, preferably democratic, government takes over.

Bringing democracy to Iraq

Then there is Iraq. [Iraqi leader] Saddam Hussein is a despised figure whose people rose up in rebellion in 1991 when given the opportunity to do so by American military victories. But the first Bush administration refused to go to Baghdad, and stood by as Saddam crushed the Shiite and Kurdish rebellions. As a shameful moment in U.S. history, the abandonment of these anti-Saddam rebels ranks right up there with our abandonment of the South Vietnamese in 1975. We now have an opportunity to rectify this historic mistake.

To turn Iraq into a beacon of hope for the oppressed peoples of the Middle East: Now that would be a historic war aim.

The debate about whether Saddam Hussein was implicated in the September 11 attacks misses the point. Who cares if Saddam was involved in this particular barbarity? He has been involved in so many barbarities over the years—from gassing the Kurds to raping the Kuwaitis—that he has already earned himself a death sentence a thousand times over. But it is not just a matter of justice to depose Saddam. It is a matter of self defense: He is currently working to acquire weapons of mass destruction that he or his confederates will unleash against America and our allies if given the chance.

Once Afghanistan has been dealt with, America should turn its attention to Iraq. It will probably not be possible to remove Saddam quickly without a U.S. invasion and occupation—though it will hardly require half a million men, since Saddam's army is much diminished since the Gulf War, and we will probably have plenty of help from Iraqis, once they trust that we intend to finish the job this time. Once we have deposed Saddam, we can impose an American-led, international regency in Baghdad, to go along with the one in Kabul. With American seriousness and credibility thus restored, we will enjoy fruitful cooperation from the region's many opportunists, who will show a newfound eagerness to be helpful in our larger task of rolling up the international terror network that threatens us.

Over the years, America has earned opprobrium in the Arab world for its realpolitik backing of repressive dictators like Hosni Mubarak and the Saudi royal family. This could be the chance to right the scales, to establish the first Arab democracy, and to show the Arab people that America is as committed to freedom for them as we were for the people of Eastern Europe. To turn Iraq into a beacon of hope for the oppressed peoples of the Middle East: Now that would be a historic war aim.

Ambitious goals

Is this an ambitious agenda? Without a doubt. Does America have the resources to carry it out? Also without a doubt. Does America have the will? That is an open question. But who, on December 6, 1941, would have expected that in four years' time America would not only roll back German and Japanese aggression, but also occupy Tokyo and Berlin and impose liberal democracy where dictators had long held sway? And fewer American lives were lost on December 7, 1941, than on September 11, 2001.

"With respect to the nature of the regime in Afghanistan, that is not uppermost in our minds right now," Secretary of State Colin Powell recently said. If not uppermost, though, it certainly should be on our minds. Long before British and American armies had returned to the continent of Europe—even before America had entered the struggle against Germany and Japan—Winston Churchill and Franklin Roosevelt met on a battleship in the North Atlantic to plan the shape of the postwar world. The Atlantic Charter of August 14, 1941, pledged Britain and America to creating a liberal world order based on peace and national self-determination. The leaders of America, and of the West, should be making similar plans today.

Once they do, they will see that ambitious goals—such as "regime change"—are also the most realistic. Occupying Iraq and Afghanistan will hardly end the "war on terrorism," but it beats the alternatives. Killing bin Laden is important and necessary; but it is not enough. New bin Ladens could rise up to take his place. We must not only wipe out the vipers but also destroy their nest and do our best to prevent new nests from being built there again.

12

The United States Should Seek Alternatives to Military Force in Responding to Terrorism

Craig Eisendrath

Craig Eisendrath is a senior fellow at the Center for International Policy in Washington, D.C., and the author of The Phantom Defense: America's Pursuit of the Star Wars Illusion.

The United States responded to the attacks of September 11, 2001, with unilateral military force. Rather than responding to future terrorist threats the same way, the United States should work to forge an international coalition against terrorism. America should return to the multilateral approach it embraced briefly at the end of World War II. It should work with the United Nations to create an international deployment force, an international criminal court, a worldwide arms control program, and better policies for aiding world economic and social development and human rights. The alternative—continued military action in countries around the world—will only increase other nations' hostility toward the United States, curtail progress in those nations, and ultimately result in more terrorist threats.

When the U.S. answered the September 11, 2001, terrorist attacks with unilateral military force, it appeared at the time to be the only option America had. Critics suggested that multilateral action might have made more sense, but the timeline for its possible crafting through the United Nations seemed to stretch out indefinitely, and the American public would brook little delay.

Declaring a state of war in response to what seemed clearly to be an international criminal action also seemed off the mark, but was there an alternative? Declaring that, if terrorists Osama bin Laden, his lieutenants,

Craig Eisendrath, "U.S. Foreign Policy After September 11," *USA Today*, vol. 130, May 2002, p.12.

or Muhammad Omar were caught alive, they would be tried by a U.S. military tribunal ran the risk of further alienating the Islamic world and violating due process, but here again, was there an alternative?

President George W. Bush and his administration have repeatedly stated that the war on terrorism will last decades and that Americans are possibly entering into a period of international chaos. At the same time, his administration is doing nothing to change this world, so that, if 9/11 occurred again, the U.S. would be limited to the same options.

Is there an alternative? Could America help build a world in which the threat of terrorism was significantly reduced, and, if such an act occurred, could it be handled better? Such an option would necessitate a radical change in U.S. foreign policy, one based on cooperative multilateral relations, not erratic and unilateral displays of power with only passing nods to international cooperation.

To support such a policy, the U.S.'s intelligence system and foreign policy establishment would need to be far more aware of the desperate needs and discontents of other nations and peoples than they have been. With this awareness, the events of Sept. 11 might have been anticipated and possibly prevented, and American foreign policy transformed to reconstruct a world in which terrorism would be far less likely.

A multilateral approach

Such a foreign policy would contain a number of key elements: ready UN deployment force, a standing criminal court, a comprehensive arms control regime, a responsible program for world economic and social development, and an enforced minimum international standard of human rights.

This was the vision of the world that the U.S. held briefly at the end of World War II. This is the vision to which it needs to return if it is to do better than frantically respond to a future of almost predictable provocation.

At the end of World War II, America took the lead in establishing the UN. The League of Nations and the collective security arrangements prior to the war had proven inadequate, and there were those in its final days who felt the world had been washed clean by its suffering and might just possibly be ready to embrace a new collective order.

A ready UN deployment force. With the wartime alliance still intact, the UN Charter, under Chapter VII, outlined how the world organization could mobilize a force based on contributions from member states acting on decisions of the Security Council. The Charter, while not directly outlining a ready deployment force, looked in this direction. Air force contingents were to be held "immediately available," a standing Military Staff Committee was envisaged, and other provisions suggested the creation of ready units. However, by the end of 1947, with the Cold War already a reality and the wartime alliance in pieces, cooperation through the Security Council was no longer possible, at least on issues affecting East-West conflicts.

Throughout the 1940s and 1950s, with Western Europe and the Latin American republics firmly in the U.S.'s camp, and United Nations membership less than a quarter of what it is today, the U.S. enjoyed what American diplomats called the "automatic majority." If the U.S. were blocked by veto in the Security Council, it could organize effective UN action through the General Assembly, as it did under the "United for Peace"

Resolution during the Korean War. In the 1950s, the U.S. also backed UN peacekeeping, particularly in the Middle East, with operations like the 1956 United Nations Emergency Force.

The advantages of working through the United Nations were clear. The aim of U.S. policy to diffuse international tensions, such as in the Middle East or Congo, could be effected without the direct use of American troops or, indeed, those from any of the major powers. The troops on the ground could come from countries that, in the dispute in question, would be neutral and nonthreatening. The logistical and financial support could come from powers, like the U.S., able to provide it, without the political consequences of great-power involvement.

The U.S. has maintained its role as the world's major supplier of small arms and has continued to produce bacteriological weapons.

With entrance into the United Nations in the late 1950s and 1960s of the former colonial powers and the reality that the U.S. could be outvoted, particularly in the area of economic and social policy, America ended its romance with the UN. I remember as a young Foreign Service Officer, working in the United Nations Political Office of the State Department, the increasing difficulty of gaining clearance for UN actions from the geographic bureaus of the State Department and other agencies in the U.S. government. This detachment from the UN increased over the next two decades, particularly during the Republican administrations of Ronald Reagan and George H.W. Bush.

Despite some clear success in UN peace-keeping, such as the operation in Cyprus in preventing the two sides from aggravated conflict or the mediating work in El Salvador allowing that country to emerge from a destructive civil war, the U.S. saw it as an increasingly unlikely option. Problems in the UN's unpreparedness to meet a quickly developing conflict and its lack of resources were allowed to fester due to inadequate U.S. leadership and financial support.

Following the Republican takeover of Congress in 1994 by what have been called the "defense hawks," backed up by conservative think tanks such as the Hoover Institute, Heritage Commission, and the American Enterprise Institute, unilateralism became the guiding philosophy of American foreign policy. Disaffection with the UN resulted in the direct withholding of dues and a continuing U.S. refusal to cooperate with any plan to establish standby deployable forces. While, following Sept. 11, the Bush Administration finally paid up most of America's back dues and has given lip service to selective international cooperation, it still has not supported the idea of a ready deployment force.

What a difference such a force might have made. In Rwanda, for example, dispatch of effective forces could have ended any possibility of the Tutsi genocide; in Somalia, it would have made U.S. intervention unnecessary; and in Congo, it might have stopped a war that has resulted in hundreds of thousands of deaths. In Afghanistan, the availability of UN forces could have obviated the need for unilateral U.S. action and established a totally different precedent for dealing with international terrorism. The fact that a seasoned ready deployment force did not exist gave logic to American unilateral moves which would otherwise have been unnecessary.

An international criminal court. The same logic applies to the U.S. decision to try terrorists by American military tribunals. Following World War II, the U.S. took the lead in establishing the Nuremberg trials, in which leading Nazis were tried and condemned as international criminals and brought to justice. It was in those trials that the concept of crimes against humanity was defined, and the concept of international criminal law provided a solid precedent.

With the retreat of the U.S. from multilateral involvement, Washington dragged its feet on efforts to establish an effective international juridical process. During the 1980s contra war in Nicaragua, for instance, the U.S. refused to recognize the decision of the International Court of Justice that America had illegally mined the harbor in Managua. Although the U.S. has supported the international war crimes tribunal in the Hague bringing Serbian leader Slobodan Milocevic to justice for atrocities in Kosovo, Bosnia, and Croatia, it has refused to adhere to the International Criminal Court. U.S. objections, rather than being the basis of negotiations, have led to a flat refusal to adhere.

America's refusal, and the consequent loss of confidence-building experience which such a court might have amassed, has, according to the Bush Administration, left it with no option in dealing with terrorists like Osama bin Laden except a trial in the U.S. and, particularly, a closed military tribunal. Where conviction in an open and fair trial of crimes against humanity before an international court might carry weight in the Islamic world, such a result in a closed and suspect U.S. military tribunal would make a martyr of bin Laden or any future terrorist.

Arms control. In still another area, that of arms control, American unilateralism has left the U.S. at a huge disadvantage in dealing with the post–Sept. 11 world. American disaffection with arms control reverses U.S. policy initiated at the end of World War II.

Wouldn't an economic aid program be more effective in curbing long-range terrorist threats than the tens of billions of extra dollars America is pouring into the regular-military budget?

Following the dropping of nuclear bombs on Hiroshima and Nagasaki, the U.S. proposed the international control of nuclear weapons with the Baruch Plan, and for the next 40 years was the lead proponent of verifiable arms control agreements. These agreements—such as the Limited Test Ban of 1963, the Non-Proliferation Pact of 1967, the Anti-Ballistic Missile Treaty of 1972, and the Strategic Arms Limitation Treaties of 1974 and 1979—have made the world a far safer place than it would have been without them.

This process of limiting arms would seem to be continuing, most recently in the negotiations between Bush and Russian President Vladimir Putin, resulting in an agreement to reduce deliverable nuclear warheads to somewhere between 1,700 and 2,200. However, with a 10-year period for the reduction and the possibility of storing, not destroying, the warheads, the results have been less than exciting, despite a public relations hype which would indicate more substantial progress.

U.S. hypocrisy

However, on March 9, 2002, a secret Pentagon report, the *Nuclear Posture Review*, called for the use of a wide range of nuclear weapons against nonnuclear countries such as Iraq, Iran, North Korea, Syria, and Libya. It also envisions the U.S. threatening nuclear retaliation in case of "an Iraqi attack on Israel or its neighbors, or a North Korean attack on South Korea, or a military confrontation over the status of Taiwan." By calling upon the U.S. to develop new nuclear weapons designed to penetrate underground bunkers, it suggests the resumption of underground testing. Widening of the use of nuclear weapons and possible resumption of testing would seriously threaten the present moratorium on the use of nuclear weapons, foster nuclear proliferation, and undermine world security.

This report is simply the most recent of a long series of efforts by the Bush Administration to undermine the arms control regime. In general, it has opposed any international agreements which would restrict U.S. military options. It has willfully wrecked international negotiations looking to control bacteriological weapons, backed off from agreements restricting small arms and land mines, refused adherence to the Comprehensive Test Ban Treaty, and unilaterally abrogated the 1972 Anti-Ballistic Missile (ABM) Treaty, the first such pact to be abrogated by a major power. It has also reduced its support for the Nunn-Lugar program controlling Russian nuclear materials and technology. At the same time, the U.S. has maintained its role as the world's major supplier of small arms and has continued to produce bacteriological weapons and, with the other nuclear powers, refused to denuclearize itself in conformity to the 1967 Non-Proliferation Pact.

The result is a world in which proliferation of nuclear, bacteriological, and chemical weapons is far more likely, and one wherein these and conventional weapons will predictably fall into the hands of terrorists. It makes no sense to decry terrorists and then fail to adhere to international agreements limiting their access to weapons. Nor does it make any sense to fail to comply with the Comprehensive Test Ban Treaty, then decry the development of nuclear arsenals by India and Pakistan, with the sharp possibility, with the conflict over Kashmir festering between them, that these weapons will be used within the next decade. Nor does it make any sense to abrogate the ABM Treaty, yet seek adherence of other countries to arms control agreements.

In outer space, the U.S. has stood virtually alone in refusing to comply with UN resolutions seeking international agreement on the deweaponization of space, and it is vigorously pursuing development of a wide range of space-based weapons, including laser and kinetic ones. "Full-spectrum dominance" in the phrase used by the U.S. Space Command, is a virtual invitation to weapons competition and space terrorism, as well as the costly replication of the U.S. Global Positioning System by the European Union, Russia, and China.

Again, a major reversal of American policy, involving adherence to multilateral systems of control and deweaponization of space, seems clearly in order. The U.S. must continue to maintain outer space as a sanctuary, not the newest arena for an international arms race. Equally, the Administration must not indulge itself in the religious logic of unilateralist missile defense, or the shabby need to pay off defense contractor debts, by deploying a system that has little justification in view of existing international threats, little possibility of working, and a large chance of fostering an international arms race.

The U.S. must also reconsider its stance on the Comprehensive Test Ban Treaty. Being the world's one superpower, it can well accept the inhibitions of testing nuclear weapons, as its technology exceeds that of any possible competitors. The Bush Administration must reconsider its stance on small arms, bacteriological weapons, and land mines as well.

Dealing with the causes of terrorism

Economic and social development. It is not enough to crash terrorism militarily, as it can operate despite significant military losses. What is necessary is to change the environment in which terrorism thrives. Similar thinking lay behind the Marshall Plan following World War II. Ultimately, $12,000,000,000 in U.S. funds were spent on the reconstruction of Europe. The lesson had been learned from World War I that economic and social instability gives rise to international security threats. A Nazi Germany would be inconceivable without the ruinous inflation and depression following the war. As a remedy, the Marshall Plan was a huge success. Not only was Soviet communism contained, but Western Europe emerged prosperous and hopeful, and thereby democratic.

As the former colonial areas nationalized, momentum in the U.S. for providing needed economic aid tapered off. From being the world's most-generous developed nation, America dropped to the bottom of the list, with more and more of its dwindling aid package going to specific strategic countries, such as Israel and Egypt, and to military aid. The U.S. has virtually ignored Africa, as well as large areas of the former Soviet Union. This policy of neglect has permitted continuing misery in Central America and parts of Asia, and, despite pleas from UN Secretary General Kofi Annan, an international AIDS crisis is being met with disgracefully little help from the U.S.

Human rights under multilateral auspices offers another way terrorism can be contained.

America needs to reassess its stance. Is it more cost-effective to build a national missile defense system to stop North Korea at a price of $150–300,000,000,000, or to provide that impoverished nation with economic aid, encouragement to negotiate its differences with South Korea, and access to international technology, such as communication satellites? Congress, though, does not consider the relative cost-effectiveness of military vs. diplomatic and economic programming.

Such thinking, however, should be applied to the U.S.'s present policy in the Middle East. Dollar for dollar, wouldn't an economic aid program be more effective in curbing long-range terrorist threats than the tens of billions of extra dollars America is pouring into the regular-military budget, particularly as these increases were mainly drawn up before Sept. 11 and have little to do with terrorism? Doesn't considering relative cost-effectiveness make sense?

With an imaginative aid program in the Middle East, the U.S. could significantly change the environment in which terrorism thrives. Terrorists recruited from educated classes are generally young men who see no useful social role for themselves in their own countries. The recruits for terrorist armies, such as the Pakistanis who volunteered for the Taliban, are often drawn from the hopeless poor. Both classes could be absorbed into effective economic development, and with the growth of the middle class would come the democratic political structures that are antithetical to the formation of terrorism.

Such an aid program in the Middle East, or in Africa, would need to work with a radically different base than did the Marshall Plan in the 1940s. Corrupt, ineffectual, and dictatorial governments, and the lack of a basic infrastructure and skilled population, present formidable problems. These, however, are not reasons to avoid economic aid; they are, rather, reasons to put America's best thinking to design programs that can work.

Human rights

Human rights under multilateral auspices offers another way terrorism can be contained. As in other areas, the U.S.'s retreat from multilateral involvement since the end of World War II has weakened its options.

In 1948, the U.S. took the lead in the drawing up of the Universal Declaration of Human Rights. The thinking was that, despite permissible differences in cultures, certain human rights were basic, including proscriptions against cruel, inhuman, or degrading punishment; equality before the law; protection against arbitrary arrest, detention, or exile; the right to a fair court trial; and the right of free movement and asylum. The bottom line was the basic right to live or—perhaps more accurately—the right to personal security.

In the decades that followed, a strong case was made that gross violation of human rights should result in the international community invoking sanctions, including military force. Such "humanitarian intervention" would be an obligation not only in areas under oppressive national governments, but where national jurisdictions either did not apply or were not effective. In short, all people on the planet would be the charge or ward of the United Nations, much as small children are the wards of states. The state need not prescribe how they should be brought up if they are adequately fed, housed, and schooled. Cultural differences are respected, but, if those youngsters are beaten, starved, or molested, it has the obligation to intervene.

In the decades following the Universal Declaration, though, the U.S. frustrated international efforts to create an enforceable standard on the basis that its own violations of the rights of minorities, particularly Native Americans and African-Americans, might be called into question. What was Washington afraid of—rectifying long-standing abuses that ran counter to the Constitution and Bill of Rights?

Had such a system of international enforcement been in place, the United Nations would have acted years ago, possibly as early as 1996, in stopping the Taliban from its shameful treatment of women, in clear violation of the Universal Declaration. The situation the U.S. faced on Sept. 11 might well have never occurred, and in many areas of the world, the threat of humanitarian intervention might well deter governments from gross violations of human rights.

In the end, there is no guarantee, even with adequate multilateral machinery in place, that some madman will not throw a bomb or send an anthrax letter. Neither is this to minimize that cultural differences fostering fundamentalist Islamic hatred may in some instances simply be intractable. Still, in a world knit together with multilateral agreements and cooperative projects, the possibility of a continuous supportive environment for terrorism severely diminishes.

Clearly, such a world serves American security interests better than one in which the U.S. sets the precedent for the unilateral use of force, and otherwise turns away from multilateral cooperation. It also reflects the globalization of the economy, the dominant fact of the post–World War II world. Unilateralism looks backwards to a world of sovereign states that emerged in the 17th century and is now being phased out. The interconnectedness of global economic relations logically requires a parallel political structure.

The option to use military force, particularly unilateral force, ups the ante for competing states and forces them to divert needed resources toward arms as opposed to economic and social problems. It thereby increases the risk of political instability and terrorism. At the same time, increased military budgets divert funds in the U.S. from domestic priorities such as health and education, and thereby reduce the quality of life in America.

The creation of a world based on multilateral cooperation, and in which America takes its global responsibilities more seriously, reflects the U.S.'s deepest values. America can live in a realpolitik world where a narrow interpretation of the U.S.'s national interest allows it to see the needs of other people on this planet as having no moral hold on American policies. In the end, though, the nation knows it is wrong. If the U.S. is truly committed to the morality that Americans express in their churches, mosques, and synagogues, Washington has no other choice but to widen its scope and deal with the planet as a single unit. The globalization of the economy must be paralleled by the globalization of American morality and reflected in the U.S.'s foreign policy. Multilateralism holds the key to a more-secure and humane future.

13

The United States Should Not Use Military Force to Take Control of Vital Resources in the Middle East

John M. Swomley

John M. Swomley is a professor of social ethics at St. Paul School of Theology in Kansas City, Missouri.

America's heavy reliance on the use of military force in its "war on terrorism" may be part of a larger effort to expand its global military and economic empire. For example, the military bases created in Afghanistan during the war against terrorism could eventually enable the United States to build an oil pipeline to the Indian Ocean. America's proposed invasion of Iraq—which would surely kill thousands of innocent civilians—may also be motivated by the prospect of gaining control over Iraqi oil fields. Meanwhile, the U.S. media has downplayed the number of civilian casualties in Afghanistan as well as the ethical and constitutional problems raised by President George W. Bush's proposal to conduct a "preemptive strike" against Iraq.

The events of September 11, 2001, are said to have changed every thing. George W. Bush announced that the United States would declare war against any nation harboring terrorists and sent U.S. armed forces into Afghanistan to oust the Taliban [ruling regime], eliminate al-Qaeda, and catch Osama bin Laden. Not only did a sense of foreboding pervade the U.S. population but it was fostered by the media. Following the attacks in New York and Washington, Dan Rather, anchor of *CBS Evening News*, said, "George Bush is the president. He makes the decisions. Whenever he wants me to line up, just tell me where. And he'll make the call."

The U.S. Catholic bishops as a body announced publicly their vote— 267 to 4—to support the war in Afghanistan. As reported in the *Jesus Jour-*

John M. Swomley, "Parlaying Tragedy into Empire," *Humanist*, vol. 62, September/October 2002. Copyright © 2002 by the American Humanist Association. Reproduced by permission.

nal, "Most of the heads of the other monotheistic religions in the United States," from Billy Graham on down, didn't mince words "about their desire to give spiritual and conscience comfort to the American war effort."

Throughout the ensuing war, Americans have received no official reports of the civilian casualties in Afghanistan, as Secretary of Defense Donald Rumsfeld, accompanied by men in uniform, brief the press and the population. Only *Extra!*—the magazine of Fairness and Accuracy in Reporting—reported that there may be over 3,500 civilian deaths and that "both Amnesty International and Human Rights Watch have voiced strong concern about the loss of civilian lives and separately called for a moratorium on the use of cluster bombs."

[The war on terrorism] will lead to an even greater U.S. military occupation of the world and . . . to a U.S. "garrison state."

Agence France Presse noted on December 6, 2001, that refugees from Kandahar "spoke of tremendous civilian casualties" when wave after wave of U.S. bombers targeted the city. It further reported that "two months of relentless bombardment have reduced the city of Kandahar to a ghost town," with no water or electricity, scarce food, and "housing only [for] the famished who were too poor to leave."

What has the war accomplished? It hasn't led to the capture of [the terrorist alleged to have masterminded the September 11 attacks] Osama bin Laden, who as recently as July 10, 2002, is reported alive and well. It liberated Afghanistan from Taliban rule, but it hasn't stopped terrorism—as evidenced by the assassination of the interim government's vice-president. It hasn't eliminated the al-Qaeda, pockets of which continue to mount armed resistance and to issue threats of future violence against the American people. In fact, if the frequent Bush administration alerts about impending terrorist attacks aren't simply psychological ploys to maintain citizen support for Bush's war policies, the war in Afghanistan has increased rather than decreased threats of terrorism.

A war for oil?

While the war in Afghanistan and the attacks of September 11 dominated television, radio, and print media, it is important to view these events in a wider context. Bruce Cumings of the University of Chicago has written, "Despite the mainstream media's verdict on the great success of the war, it will lead to an even greater U.S. military occupation of the world and hence to a U.S. 'garrison state.'" Cumings notes in the March 4, 2002, *Nation* the Pentagon's announcement of a new commitment to bases in Central Asia—"an air base near Bishtek, the capital of Kyrgzstan, that would hold up to 3,000 troops; massive upgrading of existing military bases and facilities in Uzbekistan . . . and Pakistan" where several bases now house U.S. forces with next-to-no media access or scrutiny; creation and expansion of remaining military bases in Afghanistan and other "airfields in locations on the perimeter of Afghanistan."

Uri Averney, former member of the Israeli Knesset and activist for peace and international affairs, wrote in the Israeli journal *Ma'ariv* in February 2002:

> If one looks at the map for the big American bases created for the war, one is struck by the fact that they are completely identical to the route of the projected oil pipeline to the Indian Ocean.

He is evidently referring to a projected oil line planned by a Texas oil company prior to the September attacks.

When Cumings referred to the "garrison state" he was pointing to the fact that the United States has already left troops and bases in every country in which it has ever fought: 37,000 in South Korea after the war in 1953; armed forces in Germany, Japan, and Okinawa since World War II; and 5,000 in Saudi Arabia since the Gulf War. In addition, the United States maintains virtual control over the Pacific Ocean, with bases stretching from Australia to Alaska, and a major sphere of influence in Europe through the North Atlantic Treaty Organization (NATO). The United States also has other bases in the Middle East, such as Bahrain.

The . . . Bush administration's solution to . . . [America's] "contradiction of imperial growth and domestic decay is to conquer overseas countries with vital resources."

One could almost say that the United States rules the world—if, in addition to being the world's military superpower, we add its financial dominance worldwide. According to an analysis by James Petras in the June 2002 *Z Magazine:* "Almost 48 percent of the largest companies and banks are U.S., 30 percent from the European Union and 10 percent are Japanese." Moreover, he adds, U.S. companies are

> the dominant force in finance, pharmaceutical, biotech, information, software and retail trade. The concentration of U.S. economic power is even more evident if we look at the top 10 companies in the world. 90 percent are U.S.-owned. Of the top 25, 75 percent are U.S.-owned, and of the top 100, 57 percent are U.S.-owned.

It is even more significant that Africa, China, and Latin American countries aren't among the major owners. And Asia is virtually absent, with only "three companies among the top 500, less than one percent."

There are liabilities to this economic empire—such as the increased cost of military supremacy; arrogance and irresponsibility of, even fraud by, corporate executives; tax cuts for the rich which have stimulated overseas investments and added to the budget deficit. A major result, according to Petras, is that this huge overseas empire has caused "a trade deficit this year approaching the unsustainable level of one-half trillion dollars."

Petras points out that the George W. Bush administration's solution to this "contradiction of imperial growth and domestic decay is to conquer overseas countries with vital resources." These countries—including Afghanistan, Iran, Iraq, and some former Soviet republics which either border on the oil-rich Caspian Sea or have other oil potential—are one explanation of the Bush–Dick Cheney reference to Iraq and Iran as part of their "axis of evil."

In fact, a document leaked to the *New York Times* outlines the logistics of a possible all-out invasion of Iraq. According to Jonathan Marcus of the BBC:

> The U.S. Central Command document cited in [the *New York Times*] is not a final war plan—rather a concept of operations. It sets out in broad terms what the battle to topple Saddam Hussein might look like. . . . The U.S. military seem to be envisaging a sort of Desert Storm II—similar in some ways to the original Gulf War. . . . This would be a vast operation involving a concerted air, sea, and land assault from the north, the south, and the west.

However, Stephanie Reich points out in the spring 2002 issue of the *Covert Action Quarterly* (founded more than twenty-two years ago to document U.S. intelligence activities both at home and abroad) that outgoing Secretary of Defense William Cohen advised the Bush administration that "Saddam Hussein's forces are in a state where he cannot pose a threat to his neighbors." And Scott Ritter, an outspoken former marine and a United Nations weapons inspector, affirmed Cohen's assessment. But, as Reich also notes, "There are more than seventy known oil fields in Iraq, only fifteen of which have been developed."

Exaggerated threats

The *Covert Action Quarterly* also contains a six-page discussion of Israeli and U.S. allegations that Iraq's weapons pose a serious military threat. It points out that it was Israel, not Iraq, that introduced nuclear and chemical weapons into the region and further argues that Saddam Hussein had "advanced an alternative: the transformation of the entire Middle East into a nuclear, chemical, and biological weapons-free zone." Iraq also signed a Non-Proliferation Treaty—information not widely known. The *Quarterly* notes, "According to several UN inspectors, Iraq no longer has any weapons of mass destruction; nor could Iraq purchase the components of these weapons under the present sanctions."

In view of these facts, it is surprising that so many independent newspapers and even such leading journals as the *New Yorker* (March 25, 2002), the *Atlantic Monthly* (May 2002), *Vanity Fair* (April 2002), and *Time* (May 13, 2002) are encouraging the Bush administration to carry out its threat of a bloody assault on the people of Iraq.

Finally, there has been little alarm or opposition expressed to Bush's advocacy of first-strike war. As discussed on June 1 on the *NewsHour with Jim Lehrer* and reported on June 2 by numerous media across the country, Bush told graduating cadets at West Point:

> New threats require new thinking. Deterrence . . . means

nothing against shadowy terrorist networks with no nation or citizens to defend. Containment is not possible when unbalanced dictators with weapons of mass destruction can deliver those weapons on missiles or secretly provide them to terrorists' allies. . . . We must take the battle to the enemy, disrupt his plans, and confront the worst threats before they emerge. And our security will require all Americans to be forward-looking and resolute, to be ready for preemptive action when necessary to defend our liberty and to defend our lives. . . . We are in a conflict between good and evil and America will call evil by its name.

Yet, to date, none of Bush's "axis of evil" states has threatened attacks against the United States. And nothing in Bush's speech acknowledges that the U.S. Constitution requires that war must be declared by Congress. Indeed, in late July, Donald Rumsfeld asserted emphatically that congressional action isn't required, adding that involving Congress would foolishly tip off the enemy.

According to Ari Fleischer, Bush's press spokesperson, the administration is drafting a policy that would allow preemptive strikes against any country the president believes might engage in nuclear, chemical, or biological attacks. The policy probably will include the option of using nuclear weapons ourselves. The June 11, 2002, *USA Today* reports that Vice-President Dick Cheney spoke of using such weapons.

Hasn't the time come to challenge such a warped response to the events of September 11 and the assumption that threats—real or imagined—should lead to war against entire nations? Should we let such threats undermine our Constitution and destroy the liberties we have always cherished and our relatives have fought and died to preserve—and in the process murder thousands of innocent and powerless people in the countries we attack?

Organizations and Websites

The editors have compiled the following list of organizations concerned with the issues debated in this book. The descriptions are derived from materials provided by the organizations. All have publications or information available for interested readers. The list was compiled on the date of publication of the present volume; the information provided here may change. Be aware that many organizations take several weeks or longer to respond to inquiries, so allow as much time as possible.

Brookings Institution
1775 Massachusetts Ave. NW, Washington, DC 20036
(202) 797-6000 • fax: (202) 797-6004
e-mail: brookinfo@brook.edu • website: www.brook.edu

Founded in 1927, the institution conducts research and analyzes global events and their impact on the United States and U.S. foreign policy. It publishes the *Brookings Review* quarterly as well as numerous books and research papers on foreign policy. Numerous articles on the September 11, 2001, terrorist attacks on America and the war on terrorism are available on the institution's website, including "Time for the Hard Choices: The Dilemmas Facing U.S. Policy Towards the Islamic World" and "Nasty, Brutish and Long: America's War on Terrorism."

Cato Institute
1000 Massachusetts Ave. NW, Washington, DC 20001-5403
(202) 842-0200 • fax: (202) 842-3490
website: www.cato.org

The institute is a libertarian public policy research foundation dedicated to peace and limited government intervention in foreign affairs. It publishes numerous reports and periodicals, including *Policy Analysis* and *Cato Policy Review*, both of which discuss U.S. policy in regional conflicts. Addressing the war on terrorism, Cato members have published numerous analysis and opinion pieces arguing against a U.S. invasion of Iraq and for limited military action against other nations thought to support terrorism.

Center for Strategic and International Studies (CSIS)
1800 K St. NW, Washington, DC 20006
(202) 887-0200 • fax: (202) 775-3199
website: www.csis.org

CSIS is a public policy research institution that specializes in the areas of U.S. domestic and foreign policy, national security, and economic policy. The center analyzes world crisis situations and recommends U.S. military and defense policies. Its publications include the *Washington Quarterly* journal and the *Lessons of Afghanistan* and *Iraq's Military Capabilities in 2002* reports.

Council on Foreign Relations
58 E. 68th St., New York, NY 10021
(212) 434-9400 • fax: (212) 986-2984
website: www.cfr.org

The council specializes in foreign affairs and studies the international aspects of American political and economic policies and problems. Its journal *Foreign Affairs*, published five times a year, includes analyses of current ethnic conflicts around the world. Articles available on its website include "Applying the War Powers Resolution to the War on Terrorism," "War on Terrorism: World Views," and "Public Diplomacy and the War on Terrorism."

Foreign Policy Association (FPA)
470 Park Ave. South, 2nd Fl., New York, NY 10016
(212) 481-8100 • fax: (212) 481-9275
e-mail: info@fpa.org • website: www.fpa.org

FPA is a nonprofit organization that believes a concerned and informed public is the foundation for an effective foreign policy. Publications such as the annual *Great Decisions* briefing book and the quarterly *Headline Series* review U.S. foreign policy issues in China, the Persian Gulf and the Middle East, and Africa. FPA's *Global Q&A* series offers interviews with leading U.S. and foreign officials on issues concerning the Middle East, intelligence-gathering, weapons of mass destruction, and military and diplomatic initiatives.

Global Exchange
2017 Mission, #303, San Francisco, CA 94110
(415) 255-7296 • fax: (415) 255-7498
website: www.globalexchange.org

Global Exchange is a human rights organization that exposes economic and political injustice around the world. In response to such injustices, the organization supports education, activism, and a noninterventionist U.S. foreign policy. The organization believes that the terrorist attacks of September 11, 2001, do not justify U.S. retaliation against civilian populations, and it opposes a U.S. invasion of Iraq. It publishes a quarterly newsletter.

Heritage Foundation
214 Massachusetts Ave. NE, Washington, DC 20002-4999
(800) 544-4843 • (202) 546-4400 • fax: (202) 544-6979
e-mail: pubs@heritage.org • website: www.heritage.org

The foundation is a public policy research institute that advocates limited government and the free-market system. The foundation publishes the quarterly *Policy Review* as well as monographs, books, and papers supporting U.S. noninterventionism. Heritage publications on the war on terrorism include *Presidential Authority in the War on Terrorism: Iraq and Beyond*, *After the Victory: America's Role in Afghanistan's Future*, and the *Vital Role of Alliances in the Global War on Terrorism*.

Resource Center for Nonviolence
515 Broadway, Santa Cruz, CA 95060
(831) 423-1626 • fax: (831) 423-8716
e-mail: rcnv@rcnv.org • website: www.rcnv.org

The Resource Center for Nonviolence was founded in 1976 and promotes nonviolence as a force for personal and social change. The center provides speakers, workshops, leadership development, and nonviolence training programs and also publishes a newsletter, *Center Report*, twice a year.

United Nations Association of the United States of America
801 Second Ave., New York, NY 10017
(212) 907-1300
website: www.unausa.org

The association is a nonpartisan, nonprofit research organization dedicated to strengthening both the United Nations and U.S. participation in the UN Security Council. Its publications include the bimonthly newspaper the *Interdependent*, the report *Combating Terrorism: Does the U.N. Matter . . . and How*, and its statement on U.S. policy toward Iraq.

U.S. Department of State Counterterrorism Office
Office of the Coordinator for Counterterrorism, Office of Public Affairs, Room 2509, U.S. Department of State, 2201 C Street NW, Washington, DC 20520
website: www.state.gov/s/ct

This State Department is a federal agency that advises the president on the formulation and execution of foreign policy. The Office of Counterterrorism publishes the annual report *Patterns of Global Terrorism*, a list of the United States' most wanted terrorists, and numerous fact sheets, as well as news briefs and press releases on the war on terrorism.

Websites

Foreign Policy in Focus
www.fpif.org

Foreign Policy in Focus, established in 1996, seeks to make the United States a more responsible global leader and global partner. It is a "think tank without walls" that functions as an international network of more than 650 policy analysts and advocates. FPIF is committed to advancing a citizen-based foreign policy agenda—one that is fundamentally rooted in citizen initiatives and movements. FPIF members publish articles about the war on terrorism and other foreign policy topics online at the website.

International Policy Institute for Counter-Terrorism
www.ict.org.il

The institute is an Israeli-based research institute and think tank dedicated to developing innovative public policy solutions to international terrorism. The website offers profiles of terrorist organizations, a database of worldwide terrorist attacks, and numerous analysis reports. The institute's articles on state-sponsored terrorism include "The Iraqi Regime's Links to Terrorism," "State-Sponsored Terrorism: Terrorism as a Preferred Instrument of Syrian Policy," and "Iran—Terror by Proxy."

Terrorism Research Center
www.terrorism.com

The Terrorism Research Center is dedicated to informing the public of the phenomena of terrorism and information warfare. The site features essays and thought pieces on current issues, as well as links to other terrorism documents, research, and resources.

Bibliography

Books

Wlliam J. Bennett	*Why We Fight: Moral Clarity and the War on Terrorism.* New York: Doubleday, 2002.
Roger Burbach and Ben Clarke, eds.	*September 11 and the U.S. War: Beyond the Curtain of Smoke.* San Francisco, CA: City Lights Books, 2002.
Kurt M. Campbell and Michèle A. Flourney	*To Prevail: An American Strategy for the Campaign Against Terrorism.* Washington, DC: CSIS Press, 2001.
Victor Davis Hanson	*An Autumn War: What America Learned from September 11 and the War on Terrorism.* New York: Anchor Books, 2002.
Katrina vanden Heuvel, ed.	*A Just Response: The Nation on Terrorism, Democracy, and September 11, 2001.* New York: Thunder Mouth Press, 2002.
Michael A. Ledeen	*The War Against the Terror Masters: Why It Happened. Where We Are Now. How We'll Win.* New York: St. Martin's Press, 2002.
Rajul Mahajan	*The New Crusade: America's War on Terrorism.* New York: Monthly Review Press, 2002.
Richard Mintzer	*Keeping the Peace: The U.S. Military Responds to Terror.* New York: Chelsea House, 2002.
Paul R. Pillar	*Terrorism and U.S. Foreign Policy.* Washington, DC: Brookings Institution Press, 2001.
Phil Scraton, ed.	*Beyond September 11: An Anthology of Dissent.* Sterling, VA: Pluto Press, 2002.
Paul L. Williams	*Al-Qaeda: Brotherhood of Terror.* Parsippany, NJ: Alpha, 2002.
Howard Zinn	*Terrorism and War.* New York: Seven Stories Press, 2002.
Stephen Zunes	*Tinder Box: U.S. Middle East Policy and the Roots of Terrorism.* Monroe, ME: Common Courage Press, 2002.

Periodicals

America	"The Bush Doctrine," March 18, 2002.
Conrad Black	"What Victory Means," *National Interest,* Winter 2001.
Philip Bobbit	"Get Ready for the Next Long War," *Time,* September 9, 2002.
David Brooks	"A Modest Little War—an Exit Strategy Isn't a Foreign Policy," *Atlantic Monthly,* February 2002.

George W. Bush	"The 2002 State of the Union: We Will See Freedom's Victory," *Vital Speeches of the Day*, February 15, 2002.
George W. Bush	"The Coalition Against Terrorism," *Vital Speeches of the Day*, December 1, 2001.
George W. Bush	"War on Terrorism," *Vital Speeches of the Day*, December 1, 2001.
George W. Bush	"We Are at War Against Terrorism: The Attack on the Taliban," *Vital Speeches of the Day*, October 15, 2001.
Alexander Cockburn	"The Tenth Crusade," *Nation*, September 23, 2002.
David Cortright	"Proposed: A More Effective and Just Response to Terrorism," *USA Today*, January 2002.
James Fallows	"The Fifty-First State? Going to War with Iraq Would Mean Shouldering All the Responsibilities of an Occupying Power the Moment Victory Was Achieved," *Atlantic Monthly*, November 2002.
Foreign Policy	"Reinventing War," November/December 2001.
Mark Helprin	"Phony War: The President's Policy Does Not Comport with the Valor and Sacrifice of His Troops," *National Review*, April 22, 2002.
James Turner Johnson	"In Response to Terror," *First Things*, February 1999.
John F. Kavanaugh	"Militant Madness," *America*, March 25, 2002.
John Langan	"Should We Attack Iraq?: The Simplicities of Vigilant Justice Cannot Achieve Lasting Goals," *America*, September 9, 2002.
Richard Lowry	"End Iraq—to Conclude the Gulf War, Ten Years Later," *National Review*, October 15, 2001.
Richard Lowry	"Really Big Oil: While Fighting Terrorism, Fight OPEC, Too," *National Review*, December 31, 2001.
Sam MacDonald	"What Are We Marchin' For?" *Reason*, December 2001.
Mark Mazzetti	"Ready. Aim. Fire First," *U.S. News & World Report*, October 7, 2002.
Johanna McGreary	"Can Al-Qaeda Find a New Nest? To Do Their Worst, Terrorists Need a Sanctuary. The Next Order of Battle Is to Deny Them One," *Time*, December 24, 2001.
Ariel Merari	"Deterring Fear: Government Responses to Terrorist Attacks," *Harvard International Review*, Winter 2002.
Joshua Muravchick	"Hearts, Minds, and the War Against Terror," *Commentary*, May 2002.
National Journal	"A Country Guide to the War on Terrorism," October 27, 2001.

Newsweek	"A Wide World of Trouble: While Bush Pushes War Against Iraq, New Threats Loom from Al Qaeda and North Korea. Can We Fight on All These Fronts?" October 28, 2002.
William J. Perry	"Preparing for the Next Attack," *Foreign Affairs*, November/December 2001.
Kenneth M. Pollack	"Next Stop Baghdad?" *Foreign Affairs*, March/April 2002.
Progressive	"Axis to Grind," March 2002.
David Pryce-Jones	"We Are Waging a Just War," *New Criterion*, November 2001.
Kenneth Roth	"Misplaced Priorities: Human Rights and the Campaign Against Terrorism," *Harvard International Review*, Fall 2002.
Donald H. Rumsfeld	"A New Kind of War," *New York Times*, September 27, 2001.
Kenneth T. Walsh	"W, as in War," *U.S. News & World Report*, February 25, 2002.
Fareed Zakaria	"The War on Terror Goes Global," *Newsweek*, September 13, 2001.
Mortimer B. Zuckerman	"Why America Must Act," *U.S. News & World Report*, September 16, 2002.

Index